Pearls of Wisdom from Grandma

Pearls of WISDOM from Grandma

EDITED BY
JENNIFER GATES HAYES

ReganBooks
An Imprint of HarperCollins*Publishers*

PEARLS OF WISDOM FROM GRANDMA. Copyright © 1997 by Jennifer Gates Hayes. All rights reserved. Printed in the United States of America. No part of this book may be used or reproduced in any manner whatsoever without written permission except in the case of brief quotations embodied in critical articles and reviews. For information address Harper-Collins Publishers, Inc., 10 East 53rd Street, New York, NY 10022.

HarperCollins books may be purchased for educational, business, or sales promotional use. For information please write: Special Markets Department, HarperCollins Publishers, Inc., 10 East 53rd Street, New York, NY 10022.

FIRST EDITION

Designed by Laura Lindgren

Library of Congress Cataloging-in-Publication Data

Pearls of wisdom from Grandma / edited by Jennifer Gates Hayes. – 1st ed.
    p.   cm.
   ISBN 0-06-039202-9
   1. Grandmothers–Quotations. 2. Grandmothers–Miscellanea. 3. Grandparenting–Quotations, maxims, etc. 4. Grandparenting–Miscellanea. 5. Grandparent and child–Miscellanea. I. Hayes, Jennifer Gates, 1962–
HQ759.9.P43   1997
306.874'5–dc21   97-620

97 98 99 00 01 ❖/RRD 10 9 8 7 6 5 4 3 2 1

To the staff and families of
The Children's Advocacy Center of Manhattan
and in loving memory of
Mary May Bell (1906–1996)
and Maria Antonia Imprescia (1889–1972)

When a child is born, so are grandmothers.

–JUDITH LEVY, WRITER AND EDITOR

~~ —— ~~

Think not forever of yourselves, O Chiefs,
    nor of your own generation.
Think of continuing generations of our families,
    think of our grandchildren
    and of those yet unborn,
    whose faces are coming from
    beneath the ground.

–THE PEACEMAKER,
FOUNDER OF THE IROQUOIS CONFEDERACY,
CIRCA A.D. 1000

❦ WHAT A GRANDMOTHER IS ❧

A grandmother is a lady who has no children of her own, so she likes other people's little girls. A grandfather is a man grandmother. He goes for walks with the boys and they talk about fighting and traitors and [things] like that.

Grandmothers don't have to do anything except be there. They're old so they shouldn't play hard or run. It is enough if they drive us to the market where the pretend horse is and have lots of dimes ready. Or, if they take us for walks, they should slow down past things like pretty leaves or caterpillars. They should never say "Hurry Up." Usually they are fat, but not too fat to tie kids' shoes. They wear glasses and funny underwear. They can take their teeth and gums off.

It is better if they don't typewrite or play cards except with us. They don't have to be smart, only answer questions like why dogs hate cats and how come God isn't married. They don't talk baby talk like visitors do, because it is hard to understand. When they read to us they don't skip or mind if it's the same story again.

Everybody should try to have one especially if you don't have television, because grandmothers are the only grownups who have got time.

–CONTRIBUTED BY
FORMER PRESIDENT AND MRS. GEORGE BUSH,
WRITTEN ANONYMOUSLY BY AN EIGHTYEAROLD
POSTED IN A CHURCH BULLETIN

CONTENTS

Gates family portrait, circa 1910.

Her house was a conservative white on the outside. Inside, it was bright yellow, like being inside a lemon. Grandma called it "lemon," but it always reminded me of the buttercups that grew on her lawn. When the painter came and Grandma handed him the chosen paint strip, he said, "Myrl, your taste is all in your mouth," but yellow it remained. Her driveway was steep, and she always parked her 1956 Buick safely off the incline. The car was more than fifteen years old and in mint condition. After all, it had less than fifteen thousand miles on it. My dad said it was hard to rack up mileage when your travels were exclusively to and from the local Piggly Wiggly, the pharmacy, Aunt Flossie's or Doris Olson's, and occasionally the hardware store. Grandma routinely refused offers from local high school boys who coveted her pristine "antique." But she was nothing if not practical. And she had lived long enough to know better than to give up what she could count on. Those things are rare enough as it is.

In my memory, my grandmother is always waiting for us, just inside the front door pane. We are reeling from excitement and road-trip grogginess as my dad maneuvers our less-than-pristine station wagon to a spot at the curb. Doors fly open, and moments later Grandma's soft, slightly cold hands are on our faces and backs. No matter the time of day, we always arrive just in time for "supper." Supper, and food in general, was a subject Grandma took seriously. She'd set up a huge picnic table in the garage for us. At the time, I thought it was the only space that could accommodate our sprawling family, three kids and two adults. But in hindsight, it was probably the only place Grandma dared to let us eat. Her house was immaculate. Everything had its place, and only Grandma knew exactly where that was. Her floors sparkled. The picnic table was draped with a red-and-white-checked tablecloth and spread with cold cuts, soft rolls, sour pickles, special mustards, and Pringles. We ate till our small stomachs bulged, then went inside for candies. But better than the candies was what came next. My grandma settled into her deep couch, and one by one we'd crawl into her lap. Sometimes she still had her apron on, but unfailingly we'd find what we were looking for. Positioned just below her dress collar was a round pin. The circle was studded with tiny stones in different colors. "Which one am I?" we'd ask. Grandma would tug on her dress to get a better look and then begin. We held our breath as Grandma's finger touched the first stone. One by one, she pointed to our birthstones and said our names aloud. We sat quietly and listened to Grandma's voice as she gently moved around the pin, whispering the names along the circle that linked us together.

Grandmother. Few words are as evocative. It could be argued that its meaning lies as much in the name giver as in the named. Grandmothers, like beauty, lie as much in the eyes and souls of the beholder as in the women themselves. It is the gratitude, love, strength, and dreams that they inspire in their grandchildren that make them grandmothers.

This may explain why already overextended actors, political leaders, writers, directors, musicians, and athletes, as well as schoolteachers and students, single parents, and growing families found time where there often *was* none to pay tribute to the people in their own lives who carried this name. While working on this project, I fielded calls from individuals in a wide array of less-than-convenient settings–from movie sets, newsrooms, writers' rooms, and recording studios to hospital bedsides, road trips, and tropical islands. In the end, these experiences spoke nearly as loudly as the words ultimately contributed. For those who had known a rich relationship with their grandmother, the question quickly became not whether it could be done, but how.

It is difficult to imagine a social program that better demonstrates the qualities personified in the word *grand-mother* than The Children's Advocacy Center of Manhattan (CAC). It is therefore only fitting that the proceeds from this book will benefit the center. Founded in 1995, the CAC is a privately funded, nonprofit organization that provides support and resources to children and families who have experi-

Myrl Gates with her grandchildren (left to right): Kathy, Jennifer, and Alan.

enced physical or sexual abuse as well as to the community-based and social service agencies that work with them. The program was designed to reduce the trauma and eliminate the re-victimization of children following disclosure or discovery of physical or sexual abuse. The CAC is both a safe haven and an educational and resource center for children and their families who have experienced abuse and to the community at large. ReganBooks is honored to take part in a project that will help sustain this important and vital program.

This book is a collection of personal treasures whose value, in one sense, can be measured by the degree to which they are shared. Hopefully, readers will themselves become beneficiaries of the very profound humor, courage, love, compassion, bawdiness, and wisdom that brought the book into being. In this way, whether we knew our parents' mothers or not becomes less relevant. In the words of Hoh Native American Elder Leila Fisher, when a woman understands and accepts the mantle of *grandmother* and all it implies, "all children are [her] children"; her grandchildren. And across centuries and cultures, the world has been that much richer for it.

JENNIFER GATES HAYES

ACKNOWLEDGMENTS

A heartfelt thanks to my publisher, Judith Regan, who never ceases to amaze and inspire. I am grateful to her for many things but wish to thank her here for the opportunity to work on such a wonderful and meaningful project. To the incredible ReganBooks staff: my editor extraordinaire and friend, Kristin Kiser, and the incomparable David Craig, Andrew Albanese, Tom Kane, Todd Silverstein, and Angelica Canales. To BeBe Lerner at ICM for her help and input. To Georgette Mosbacher who, along with my publisher, provided the inspiration for this project and who established such a valuable and critically needed program in The Children's Advocacy Center of Manhattan. To the CAC staff, in particular executive director Susan Rios. A special thanks to Lyn Paulsin for all of her kind assistance. To my family and friends, with whom I am truly blessed: Rick Hayes; Esther and Douglas Gates; Alan and Jennifer

Gates (II); Katherine, Greg, and Emily Karlik; Margo Hayes; Tim Hayes; Laura Dickerman; John Nathan; Suzy Palitz; Joyce McFadden; Mija Strong; Jillian Medoff; and Therese Moore. A special thanks to the Epiphany School, in particular Mrs. Gates's third-grade class; Mrs. Karen Casey Gotschall's first-grade class at the Camino Real Elementary School; and to the Collegiate School. To Cathryn Girard and Caring Grandparents of America. To the HarperCollins staff: Betsy Areddy, Richard Cariello, Jane Hardick, Susan Kosko, Melanie Wertz, and to Dr. Narinder Bhalla, for their expertise.

Many thanks to Demi Moore, who so graciously supported this project, and to her talented staff: Daneen Conroy, Mark "Hunter" Reinking, Michael Hinkle, and Bonnie Camen.

And finally, to all of this book's contributors, who opened their hearts and lives and took the time to share their stories and memories.

Grandma Marie

by Demi Moore

When I think of my grand-mother, I can't help but think of home.

When I was five years old, I used to call my grand-mother up every Friday at a few minutes to five, quitting time, to tell her I was ready for my weekend pickup. So with buggy in hand and all my babies in tow, I waited curbside until she came to pick me up. I would then climb into the front seat of her (what seemed to be) enormous car and hap-pily wave good-bye to my parents, prepared to be gone and not see them the whole weekend long. Grandma's house seemed to have it all. Goodies to eat galore, with no one telling you how much is too much, as well as lots of TV, the best Sears and JCPenney catalogs to do your wish-book shopping, and unlimited back tickling and scratching until you fell asleep.

But most important, Grandma's time was my time, and there was plenty of it.

Some of my fondest childhood memories are the times spent with all my family, including aunts, uncles, and a whole slew of cousins, all crammed into my grandmother's little house with everyone sleeping every which way, with never less than two or three of us in the shower and/or the bathroom at a time, always crowding around the kitchen waiting

for one of her great home-style meals (especially the beans and cornbread), sipping sun tea and shooting the breeze. There was a great comfort in that chaos, because it was a chaos of togetherness, of belonging; and that sense of belonging was because of one person and one person only, Grandma.

Demi Moore (center) *with her grandmother Marie Hanson* (left) *and her Great-Grandma Metcalf.*

(Left to right) *Demi Moore's mother, Grandma Marie, Great-Grandma Metcalf, and Demi.*

One of my greatest desires is to be a grandmother. I can think of few accomplishments greater, actually, than fulfilling that role in a child's life. I only know how important my own grandmother has been to me, and I can only hope that I will be given that same opportunity to give back to my children's children. I hope that when my turn does come, I can show the same grace, courage, strength, and unconditional love that my grandmother has given me. It's hard to imagine having lived my life without her, because directly or indirectly I am who I am because of this woman. She would probably be surprised to know that she has affected me so much, without even trying; by doing nothing more than just being herself. But the optimum word here is *grand,* and that, my grandmother is.

GIVING

Ada Merchant holding her granddaughter Natalie.

Ada Merchant

BY NATALIE MERCHANT,
SINGER, SONGWRITER, AND MUSICIAN

Ada Merchant was a woman who existed somewhere between two distinct worlds and traditions. Although my grandmother lived in America for over seventy years, one foot remained firmly rooted in the soil of a small island in the Mediterranean Sea. She was Sicilian in blood and temperament. Her first language was a musical dialect of Italian.

Roman Catholicism was her unquestioning faith. To me, she was very much a visitor to this country from an exotic and distant land. She had survived the steerage passage, Ellis Island, English, the worsted mills, marriage, childbirth, twelve American presidents, the Great Depression and two World Wars, but in spite of the velocity of change, my grandmother remained faithful to her traditional ways and views. She was my bridge to the Old World, which I gratefully traveled across.

Throughout my childhood she was the calm, steady eye in the cyclone of events surrounding us. Outside, the atomic mushroom cloud was gathering. A lunar space module was touching down. Cities burned on television during a summer of violence. Young boys were killed in the jungles while others clashed with riot police. My father left home. My mother left the church. Life moved at an incomprehensible speed before my young eyes. But in my grandmother's kitchen there was stillness, the room was filled with the scent of coffee on the boil and bread in the oven. There was always a gathering of people. I would sit for hours at the kitchen table while my sweet aging aunts would share gossip or memories of their childhood. Neighbors would appear at the screen door with gifts of freshly picked tomatoes from their backyard gardens. Dear friends of the family would greet them with open arms. This was a peaceful and welcoming place where I belonged.

My grandmother worked tirelessly around the house and garden. It was from my grandmother I learned "the domestic arts," or "housework" as it is otherwise known. The drudgery I was expected to abhor became alchemy under the spell of my grandmother's talented hands. I remember my amazement when a bowl of bread dough rose and doubled in size. She stitched colorful strands of embroidery floss into delicate flowers. She polished tarnished silverware new. Her strawberry plants thrived and bore delicious fruits under the midsummer sun. In her basement, home-canned preserves filled the shelves. Hours of work with a crochet needle yielded intricate lace table cloths.

As her little apprentice I watched and I imitated and I learned, knowing what tradition expected of me.

My grandmother's gifts were many, but her enduring presence is the most important. Years after her death, we still work quietly together. She is with me in my vegetable garden reminding me to cover the seedlings for the frost. She stands at the stove while I pour olive oil into a pan. When I set the table for guests, I feel her. When I pull a piece of linen from the clothesline on a cool summer's evening and fold it into even quarters, she is beside me. When I replace a button or stitch the hem of a dress, I feel my hand is guided. I look down and see the hand of my grandmother pushing the thread through my needle.

It is important for the elders to be willing to give wisdom and not try to direct everything. Young people see them-selves living in this world and it is their life yet to be lived.

—MAYA ANGELOU, WRITER AND POET

❧ —— ❧

Martha Adaline Ramsay Mead

BY MARGARET MEAD,
ANTHROPOLOGIST (1901–1978)

I think it was my grandmother who gave me my ease in being a woman. She was unquestionably feminine–small and dainty and pretty and wholly without masculine protest or feminist aggrievement. She had gone to college when this was a very unusual thing for a girl to do, she had a firm grasp of anything she paid attention to, she had married and had a child, and she had a career of her own. . . . So I had no reason to doubt that brains were suitable for a woman. And as I had my father's kind of mind–which was also his mother's–I learned that the mind is not sex-typed. . . . Grandma always wanted to understand things, and she was willing to listen or read until she did. There was only one subject, she decided rather fastidiously, that she did not wish to pursue. That was birth control. At eighty, she said, she did not need to know about it. . . . Throughout my childhood she talked a great deal about teachers, about their problems and conflicts, and about those teachers who could never close the schoolhouse door behind them. The sense she gave me of what teachers are like, undistorted by my own particular experience with teachers, made me want to write my first book about adolescents in such a way that the teachers of adolescents would understand it.

Grandma . . . set me to work taking notes on [my sister's] behavior–on the first words Priscilla spoke and on the way one echoed the other. She made me aware of how Priscilla mimicked the epithets and shouts hurled up and down the back stairs by the Swedish nurse and the Irish cook and of how Elizabeth was already making poetry of life. Told that her dress was ragged, she replied happily, "Yes, I's the raggedy man." I learned to make these notes with love. . . .

I t is important to use the gifts you have. I know I have beautiful eyes and I use them."

> –SUSAN EISENHOWER, POLITICAL ANALYST
> QUOTING HER GRANDMOTHER FORMER FIRST LADY
> MAMIE EISENHOWER

Grandma Moses

BY WILL MOSES,
ART GALLERY OWNER

Anna Mary Robertson Moses was great-grandmother to me–but to the rest of the world, she was the painter Grandma Moses. When she died at 101, I was still very young, so my memories of her are limited. However, there was something so unusual about her that even I, a small child, knew I should probably pay attention.

One afternoon my mother took me to visit my great-grandmother. Grandma Moses was at the height of her fame and lived with her son Forrest and his wife, Mary (my grand-father and grandmother). Though their home boasted a beautiful sun porch studio overlooking the Hoosick River, Grandma Moses preferred to paint in the laundry room. There, she was able to gracefully bypass the seemingly endless procession of well-wishers who frequented the home and get on with the work at hand.

While the adults busied themselves outside, I stole away and discovered a wooden box full of toy cars, trucks and blocks in the front hall closet. I emptied the box and scattered its contents. A battered tin truck caught my eye. I decided to thread a piece of old string through a small hole in its bumper. With the string secure, I reasoned, I could pull my prize around. But the string was badly frayed and too large for the hole. I was growing increasingly frustrated when Grandma Moses appeared. I suppose she had been returning to her paints in the laundry room when she found me. She paused for a moment and asked me how I was doing. "Not too well!" came the response. Without a word, my 99-year-old great-grandmother knelt gently down beside me and took the tattered string in her arthritic hands. She placed the string in her mouth for a moment and then carefully twisted it between her gnarled fingers. With great ease, she slipped the thread through the tiny hole in the truck's bumper and secured it with a fine knot. With a quick tug, I was happily on my way; the truck clanging close behind.

I am not sure why this event made such a lasting impression on me. Perhaps it is because it was an act of pure kindness. Nothing in that moment could have touched or pleased me more; and in that moment, Anna Mary Robertson was a grandma, *my* grandma–not Grandma Moses.

We never can predict what children will remember us for or the impact that our actions, both large and small, will have on them. Taking a moment to share love and attention with a child makes a difference for a lifetime.

I look back on my life like a good day's work, I have known nothing better and have made the best out of what life has offered. Life is what we make it, always has been, always will be.

–*GRANDMA MOSES (ANNA MARY ROBERTSON), PAINTER*

Almira Burdg Milhous

BY FORMER PRESIDENT
RICHARD MILHOUS NIXON (1913-1994)

My grandmother, Almira Burdg Milhous, lived to be ninety-four. At our traditional Christmas family reunions at her house she sat regally in her best red velvet dress as all the grandchildren brought their very modest presents to her. She praised them all equally, remarking that each was something she had particularly wanted. She seemed to take a special interest in me, and she wrote me verses on my birthday and on other special occasions. On my thirteenth birthday, in 1926, she gave me a framed picture of Lincoln with the words from Longfellow's "Psalm of Life" in her own handwriting beneath it:

> *Lives of great men oft remind us,*
> *We can make our lives sublime,*
> *And departing, leave behind us*
> *Footprints on the sands of time.*

I hung the picture above my bed at home, and it is one of my fondest possessions.

A lways buy the best you can afford, whether it's a pair of gloves or a house."

–DEBBIE KESLING, WRITER
ADVICE FROM HER GRANDMOTHER LOLA MARTIN

Elizabeth Hering Felsing

BY MARLENE DIETRICH,
ACTRESS (1901–1992)

M y wonderful and gentle grandmother ... was not only the most beautiful of all women but also the most elegant, most charming, and most perfect person that ever lived. Her hair was dark red and her eyes of an iridescent violet-blue. She was tall and slim, ever radiant and cheerful. She had married at the age of seventeen and was always taken to be as old or as young as she herself wished to appear. She wore expensive clothes and even her gloves were made to measure. She was naturally elegant and didn't concern herself with what was fashionable. She loved horses, went riding every morning very early, and sometimes she would pass by our house just before school and throw me a kiss through a veil in which the early morning air mixed with her perfume. My mother never objected to any of her decisions, even though they might lead to a reversal of my daily program. My grandmother showered me with love, tenderness, and kindness. She awakened in me the longing for beautiful things, for paintings, for Fabergé boxes, horses, carriages, for the warm, soft roseate pearls set off against the white skin of her neck, and for the rubies that sparkled on her hands.

She would let me balance her shoes on my little finger and say: "This is how light they must be." Before the war I had always impatiently awaited the French shoemaker who would come in person every season to take orders for new shoes and to deliver already ordered shoes, but I was never allowed to see him. "School is more important," she would say, "and besides, shoes are a serious matter." My grandmother was at one and the same time very real and very mysterious, a dream image, perfect, desirable, distant, and fascinating. But her love was *here,* present.

Mamie Cecil Bowling

BY CHRISTIE BRINKLEY,
MODEL AND ACTRESS

Whenever my grandma needed a quick break while babysitting my brother, Greg, and me, she would sit us both down on the kitchen floor. Then she would pop out her false teeth and put them down on the floor in front of us, warning, "Don't move or they'll bite you!" We didn't move a hair until she popped them back into her mouth and gave us a big smile. It's funny because in the warmth of her smile those teeth never looked scary.

❧ —— ❧

TO OLD AGE

*I see in you the estuary that enlarges and spreads itself
grandly as it pours in the great sea.*

—WALT WHITMAN

❧ —— ❧

Selma Mize

BY FORREST SAWYER, JOURNALIST

I come from seven generations of Floridians. Selma Mize, my maternal grandmother, came from a long line of Florida crackers. Florida was one of America's last frontiers, a fact often obscured by the dramatic settlement of the West. By the 1920s, electricity still had not made its way into central Florida.

I spent every summer with my maternal grandparents. I remember their home in central Florida as a sleepy, rural place. They lived in a crackerhouse, which was a home raised on blocks called a breezeway. The platform provided the homes much needed protection from the often fierce natural elements of central Florida. At night, we all slept outside in a screened-in area called a sleeping porch. I remember lying down on my grandparents' huge feather bed listening to the frogs. My grandmother lay beside me, smelling of talcum powder and recounting stories I never tired of hearing. My grandmother valued education. She was a teacher by trade and eventually became principal of the school where she taught. She was well read and had worked hard to put herself through Florida Southern College. She knew what stories I loved best: everything from Edgar Allan Poe's "The Pit and the Pendulum" to "The Cask of Amontillado." She recited scenes from *The Odyssey*, of the Cyclops blinded in one eye by Odysseus as he and his men escaped from the giant's cave. Initiated by my grandmother's wonderful story-telling, I learned to read early and developed a lifelong appetite for literature.

She also gave me the gift of her unconditional love. My grandmother had a way of wrapping her grandchildren up and making us feel completely safe. Even if her embrace lasted only a moment, the sense of security and safety it instilled will last a lifetime.

~❧ —— ❧~

Mary "Billie" Bernadine Ciminella

BY ASHLEY JUDD, ACTRESS

God knew what s/he was doing when s/he gave me my grandparents.

My paternal grandmother's name was Mary Bernadine Ciminella, but everyone called her Billie. Everyone, that is, but her grandchildren. To us, she was Mamaw. I had always known Mamaw was beautiful, but, recently, looking through photographs of her in her youth, I was struck by how chic and stylish she was. In every decade, Mamaw seemed to per-fectly embody the look of the day. For every year and fashion, Mamaw was the penultimate woman of her time.

Mamaw was raised in Inez, in Martin County, Kentucky, but later settled with my grandfather in Ashland in Boyd County. Martin County is coal-mining country, the site where, in 1968, President Johnson first declared his War on Poverty. It is a place where its citizens did not pay federal taxes until the sixties because tax collectors were routinely run off the land with shotguns. Boyd County, however, was also the home of Ashland Oil and, overall, had a higher per capita income than Westchester County, New York. In short, the region is a montage of social strata and economic backgrounds. Despite the fact that my grandparents came from humbler origins, they provided every stitch of clothing I wore growing up. My grandfather even postponed his retirement so that he'd be better able to provide for us. Throughout my life, if I ever needed anything, my grandparents were there. As much as our parents loved me and my sister, daily life was often chaotic. My grandparents have always been a bastion of stability and security. A lot of my confidence, direction, and motivation are a direct result of their influence. I don't know where I'd be today without them.

Each summer at Mamaw's house, we had a routine. I woke up early to find my grandmother already downstairs, wrapped in a soft bathrobe, hair neatly fluffed, busy making my breakfast. After she fed me, we planned our day based on the weather. If it looked like rain, we'd go into town. If the sun was out, we'd head off to the club, where my grandmother dropped me off to swim while my grandfather played golf. Mamaw would then head home to start getting supper ready. The ninth hole of the club's golf course offered an unobstructed view of the pool. Without fail, my grandfather would stop at the ninth hole and wave, taking a moment to admire me. I always took this opportunity to show off for him—waving and doing flips off the diving board.

After dinner, Mamaw and I would head into her bedroom. I would pile the bed with huge feather pillows, making a lovely nest in Mamaw's soft, white sheets. The bed rested next to a row of open windows. Sheer, white curtains would flutter in the evening breeze while Mamaw and I sat together, listening to the summertime sounds of cicadas, bull frogs, and crickets. To this day, I cannot hear a mourning dove without being reminded of Mamaw. Sometimes we ate bowls of Cheerios or coffee ice cream. Other times we sang ditties together.

Often, Mamaw and I played gin rummy or casino. We always told one another that she had to re-learn how to play canasta so that she could teach me, though she never did. When our card games were over, Mamaw and I agreed on a "lights out" time. I have always loved to read. Upstairs in my attic bedroom, I was allowed to read until the time Mamaw and I chose together. Sometimes, I'd get lost in my book or I was perfectly defiant and the designated hour came and went. From downstairs, Mamaw could see my light burning past my bedtime. But she never said anything to me until the next morning. And when she did, it was clear that Mamaw wasn't upset about the time. The time was arbitrary. It was that, together, we had agreed upon something and I had not held up my end of the bargain.

Only recently did I realize how extraordinary the nature of Mamaw's reprimands were, how fair, balanced, and kind. When I misbehaved, Mamaw always sat me down across from her. She looked me in the eye and told me how she felt about what I had done. She never once threatened or shamed me in any way, never once told me I was bad. She simply made it clear that by going against what we both knew was right, I had broken a bond of trust between us. No other words or punishment were needed.

The power of my grandmother's gentle lesson was never more vivid than on one late-summer afternoon, shortly before I entered the sixth grade. I was out playing in the yard when Mamaw came to break some news: I would not be returning to northern California as I had assumed, where Mom, Sister, and I had been living for two years, but would instead be going to live with my father in Lexington, Kentucky. I had not lived with him since the first grade. My life was suddenly in massive upheaval. I also knew that Mamaw disapproved of the plan. Perhaps what followed was my attempt to find consistency and order where there was none; or perhaps I wanted to create my own little world with Mamaw in it, keep her orderliness and ethics with me. What I do know is that when the time came for Mamaw to drive me to my father's house, in my possession was all of Mamaw's costume jewelry. I had stolen it from her. We drove all the way to my father's home in a rural part of Kentucky, down his long driveway along the river, and not a word was said about the contraband in my pockets. I must have thought I was home free. As I opened the car door, climbed out, and prepared to say my good-byes, Mamaw looked at me and said, "Honey, I don't understand why you took my jewelry. Those rings aren't worth much, and even if they were, it is not about the money."

Her words cut to my bones. Mamaw knew I had stolen from her but waited until the last possible second to mention it. She had wanted to give me every opportunity to come clean on my own. When Mamaw did speak, she didn't bring the matter into a moral or philosophical realm. She spoke only of our relationship, which in and of itself was pure, and of the trust that I had betrayed. And though I won't say that all rebellious urges left me in that moment, I can say with certainty that they were never again played out with Mamaw.

Today, I like to think of myself as her heir. My hair is cut short, just as Mamaw wore it when she was my age. A few years ago, when I was doing a play in New York called *Picnic*, my godmother came up to me after a performance and said, "Good golly, you have your Mamaw's body!" I had been going through an emotionally wrenching time. I remember sitting backstage in my dressing room one night feeling particularly distraught. As I lifted my hand, my eye caught my bare upper arm. This had always been my favorite part of Mamaw's body. It was the most grandmotherly part–so soft and white. She was with me, and suddenly I felt a tremendous tenderness toward myself.

Mamaw died when I was a sophomore in college. I was shocked she was gone and I mourned her very deeply. But I have always felt that grieving is another facet of worship. You won't grieve deeply if you haven't loved deeply. Over the years, I've discovered that Mamaw's legacy extends even beyond my abiding love for her. At times when I feel down or self-destructive, I think of Mamaw and how she loved me so deeply and purely, and I thus feel that I deserve to be loved, valued, and treasured. I love myself because my grandmother loved me.

❧ —— ☙

Margaret Mary Devaney

BY THERESE MOORE, PUBLISHING EXECUTIVE

Grandma attended to her morning ritual as I sat on her bed, asking question after question; loving her; wrapped in her voice and in the security of the moment. Outside her window, several birds fluttered and sang around a feeder. Dressed in a cranberry suit, pearls resting on her cushiony breast, Grandma dipped her hands into rich cream from a shiny black jar which she dotted like butter and rubbed into her smooth skin. She passed a comb gently over the fine rim of curls framing her face; her lips were coated a 1940's red. A final drop of Shalimar and Grandma was ready to greet the world. It was not vanity that preoccupied her. It was simply that there was a right way and a wrong way to do just about anything, including preparing oneself for one's grand-daughter. My grandmother was deliberate about doing everything properly even as brain cancer forced her permanently to bed.

Grandma also valued a lady's etiquette, table manners, and oft-repeated "dry as a bone" expressions. For me, she lovingly prepared lamb chops adorned with miniature chef hats and served with tiny peas and mashed potatoes. She was an expert at keeping rooms cool and dark in spite of the mid-summer's day heat. She constructed table centerpieces, heaped with polished fruit and nuts. But what perhaps impressed me most was how Grandma could identify every Northeastern bird; describing its flight pattern, favorite seed, and nesting preference. It was because of her love for her feathered friends that we, my mother and I, tried inexhaustibly to attract birds of any kind to my bedside window, as my bed became hers during her illness. It would remain Grandma's bed for the next six months.

We picked out the perfect bird feeder and hung it from a branch that reached toward my window. We filled it to the brim with an assortment of tasty seeds. Then we waited. And waited. We watched the empty feeder as the early morning light cracked red over the horizon; until the last puff of twilight faded. We were perplexed, frustrated, and then sad. But we did not give up easily. We changed the seed to a gourmet variety, the feeder was repositioned and finally replaced altogether, all with the hope of attracting birds that might offer some comfort to Grandma. That was our wish. Perhaps Grandma had more patience. She was never alone. One of us was always with her, sharing the day's events. The birds gave us something to wait for, to hold on to, something to which we could look forward.

On a Thursday afternoon in February, Grandma closed her eyes for the last time. My mother was by her side and ran downstairs to collect my sister and me so that we could say good-bye. As we climbed the stairs, we heard a lovely song swelling. Upon entering Grandma's room, we were greeted by a beautiful chorus—a rush of color—a multitude of soul-lifting birds.

They may have failed us, but the birds did not fail my grandmother.

Gigi Epstein Cutler

Morning granny, how are you? I always knew the answer:
Fine and you, she replied,
never been much better.
Take me to the zoo? I always knew the answer:
Just a moment, let me get my hat,
Then we will be off.
Can we see the lions first? I always knew the answer:
Sure thing, right this way,
soon we will be there.
Her hair as soft as silk,
Her heart even softer.
As I sit there by her side
I felt a little safer.
She knew just what I wanted then,
And know she will forever.
Her thin little silhouette
sitting by my side,
emitting the warmth of a thousand candles
as we took that ride.
She gave me all I wanted then
And give she will forever.
She leaves me just one question now,
Which has no one reply:
Why is it we all must die?
She died not dead.

—CHARLES VOS, NINTH GRADER

We're all here for a reason. It's your duty to go out there and find out what God had in mind when he created you."

–VICKY PHILLIPS, WRITER
ADVICE FROM HER GRANDMOTHER ANABELLE ENGLAND

❧ —— ☙

Evelyn Epstein

BY KATHIE LEE GIFFORD,
TALK SHOW HOST AND SINGER

Now, my grandmother–Gram–is another story altogether. She became a formidable presence in all our lives. Having held her large family together despite an absent, hard-drinking husband, Gram, even after she remarried, was stern, tough as a rock, and suffered no nonsense from anyone. . . .

In her later years, though, Gram was fun to be around, even though she may have been a little senile back then. Some of the funniest things I remember in my life are with Gram. She'd wear those old housedresses and roll down her stockings and sit there on Easter Sunday with the Easter basket right between her legs and kind of stare out around the room with this wild look in her eye. When my brother Davy graduated from Washington Bible College, one of the strictest, staunchest, most conservative schools you can find—the cheerleaders' dresses go down to their ankles—Gram was there and it was a stifling hot June day. She was always a firm believer in drinking water. So she had her brown bag and ice cubes and water, though no one figured it was water. So during this one very still moment in the outdoor ceremony, there's Gram knocking back her water, yelling into the silence, "Hot as HELL in here." We all just wanted to sink down in our chairs and die. . . .

Old Gram. Maybe *that's* where it comes from—the shooting-my-mouth-off gene, that extra saying-whatever-pops-into-my-head chromosome or whatever it is. Got that from Gram.

Dr. Hannah Seitzick-Robbins accepting her award as Woman of the Year (1972) from the New Jersey Medical Association.

Dr. Hannah Seitzick-Robbins

BY JOHN NATHAN, GRADUATE STUDENT

In 1922, my grandmother graduated from the University of Pennsylvania Medical School and shortly thereafter became the first woman doctor in Mercer County, New Jersey. In the course of her fifty-year career as an obstetrician/gynecologist, she delivered over 10,000 children into the world.

When I was a child, we used to drive down from our family home in Connecticut to visit Grandma Hannah and Grandpa Sam at their home in Trenton, New Jersey. My siblings and I all share similar memories of those visits. Our grandparents' house was stately, almost mythic in our minds, with its front porch and grand stairway in the front hall. The plush red carpet, enormous fireplace, the velvet couch (covered in plastic when *we* were guests), and antiques lent to the home a museum-like air.

Behind a door in the main hallway was a small but well-decorated waiting room, a book-lined office with dark leather furniture, and the examining room. It was the examining room that my siblings and I remember best. Once per visit, Grandma would take us on a tour of her office and bestow upon us the ultimate gift: a ride on her examining table. The

Grandma Hannah with two of her granddaughters.

table was surrounded by the medical paraphernalia necessary for her Ob/Gyn practice. Among these strange and foreign items was something I thought I recognized: a foot-high, skin-colored plastic model of an ear. (It would be fifteen years before I realized that "the giant ear" was, in fact, a model of a uterus used for patient education.) But really, the rest was all backdrop to "the magic table." One by one, we squealed as Grandma Hannah expertly worked the electric foot controls making it rise, fall and pitch forward and back. Oh, the fun her patients must be having, I thought to myself, since trips to her office guaranteed not only tender, expert care but also an adventurous carnival ride as well! Only years later would I realize the table's true function and see that we were perhaps the only ones who ever had such a good time on that "magic table."

Agnes Cronin

BY DR. JOHN (MAC REBENNACK),
MUSICIAN, SINGER, AND SONGWRITER

My grandmother was a woman who possessed unusual powers, and she passed on to me my curiosity and inclination toward spiritualism and voodoo. As I think back, I realize that if she had been born under different circumstances, she could have been a root doctor or what we in New Orleans call a reverend mother—a female spiritual healer and community leader.

One night—I was too young to remember this—Grandmother did something that really freaked everybody out. She was sitting around our dining room table when suddenly she began to "walk" the table. It was a big, heavy oak table, carved with leaves and vines and lion's-claw feet, that was made in Angola Penitentiary. The inmates used dow pins to put the table together, constructing it with the same caliber of craftsmanship you'd see on all the gaming tables and roulette wheels they made. . . . It was one heavy table; no single guy, no matter how big, could pick it up.

According to the story, my grandmother got up from her chair and put her fists on the table, and the table lifted off the ground and began wobbling across the room with Grandmother following after it. My mother and her sisters got so scared that one of them ran off to get the priest to come and exorcise her. . . .

[Grandmother] was just a little woman, and a real sweetheart, but she had the touch.

Madame Nathee Weil

BY MADAME JEANNE PROUST,
MOTHER OF WRITER MARCEL PROUST
(1871–1922)

Madame Proust advised her son Marcel on the death of his grandmother in 1889:] Think of her, by all means, and cherish her as I do: but don't let yourself go, and spend days in tears, because it's only bad for your nerves, and she wouldn't wish it. No, the more you think of her, the more it is your duty to be as she would like you to be and act as she would like you to act.

Jillian Medoff and Mary Sacks Boyar in 1965.

Mary Sacks Boyar

BY JILLIAN MEDOFF,
AUTHOR OF HUNGER POINT

There are things about my grandmother that I will never forget. She wore pearls with her nightgown; loved Egg McMuffins and milky coffee; carried her pocketbook everywhere; and cared for her children and her husband more than she ever cared for herself. She loved me unconditionally, even when I wasn't very lovable: during high school when I smoked pot and ran around with older boys who went to "nightclubs;" in college when I wore black turtlenecks and quoted Proust and thought I knew a thing or two; and during my postcollege downfall, when I found out that I didn't.

The morning after some now-forgotten boyfriend dumped me, she and I ate Egg McMuffins at McDonald's. She tried to say all the right things, but I was nineteen, excruciatingly melodramatic and inconsolable. He is *my life*, I cried to her, I *can't bear* to be without him; you just don't *understand*. She sat with me until her Egg McMuffin congealed and her milky coffee got cold. She took a bite of her Egg McMuffin and, as she ate, a piece of rubbery egg stuck to her bottom lip. I focused on the yellow egg until it fell onto the greasy wrapper. She picked at the egg, held it toward me and asked if I wanted a bite. When I said no, she ate it herself and continued to listen until I was too exhausted to talk anymore. So it's an egg clump, mixed with her saliva and my tears that is my most vivid memory of my grandmother; vivid, I suppose, but not the most painful.

Years later, she and I spent a week at my mother's house. It was the spring of 1991 and my grandmother was dying of pancreatic cancer but none of us—not even my grandmother— knew. She didn't complain once during our visit, so I was startled when I saw her doubled-over in my sister's twin bed. "I have to go to the ladies' room," she whispered and closed her eyes. I helped her into the bathroom, but after a half-hour of exhausting, nonproductive work, she asked to lie down. "I can't go," she said her voice tinged with anger. "Please let's go back to bed." When she curled up and clutched her stomach, I tentatively suggested an enema. She didn't say yes, but she didn't say no, so I grabbed a stack of towels, some pillows, and a garbage bag. I hovered over my grandmother and administered the enema, desperate to make her comfortable.

The incident is so significant for me because it was the first time in my life that my grandmother allowed herself to be taken care of. The irony about the experience is that it is only in retrospect that I get squeamish. But I've learned that when we love, the things we find the most repulsive become the most sacred: a greasy McDonald's wrapper, a chewed piece of yellow egg, a garbage bag filled with soiled towels. And there are thresholds that we cross to demonstrate this love. We hold each other's heads over toilets, we end up wrist-deep in each other's waste. Perhaps it is by crossing these thresholds without flinching that we exhibit strength, but it is in the surrender that we are most brave. So in truth, it is my grandmother, not me, who was the more fearless. And my wish for myself is that I will continue to love with the kindness, devotion, and selflessness that she taught me that afternoon.

Rosabelle Driggs

BY *LAUREL MELLIN, M.A., R.D.,*
AUTHOR OF THE SOLUTION: WINNING
WAYS TO PERMANENT WEIGHT LOSS

When I was in middle school and was learning the hard way how tenuous the teen-age social world could be, my grandmother–Grannie Driggs, as the grandkids called her–gave me what I needed: a few good words with which to stave off the taunts of neighborhood bullies.

One afternoon, I ran to Grannie after having suffered the blow of a sharp insult from the girl next door. She responded unflinchingly. She stuck out her chin and with a knowing glance said, "Just tell them, 'Oh fishcakes!'"

Though I don't recall ever actually saying it, I didn't need to. Armed with a few good words and the vision of my grandmother uttering them I felt perfectly and completely safe.

❧ —— ☙

They make my spirits soar!

–JACQUELINE KENNEDY ONASSIS
ON HER GRANDCHILDREN

❧ —— ☙

Josephine Armstrong

BY LOUIS ARMSTRONG, MUSICIAN AND SINGER (1900–1971)

One day when I was getting water along with the rest of the neighbors on James Alley an elderly lady who was a friend of Mayann's [Louis' mother] came to my grandmother's to tell her that Mayann was very sick and that she and my dad had broken up again. My mother did not know where Dad was or if he was coming back. She had been left alone with her baby—my sister Beatrice—with no one to take care of her. The woman asked my grandmother if she would let me go to Mayann and help out. Being the grand person she was, grandma consented right away to let me go to my mother's bedside. With tears in her eyes she started to put my little clothes on me.

"I really hate to let you out of my sight," she said. "I'm so used to having you now."

"I am sorry to leave you, too, granny," I answered with a lump in my throat. "But I will come back soon, I hope. I love you so much, grandma. You have been so kind and so nice to me, taught me everything I know: how to take care of myself, how to wash myself and brush my teeth, put my clothes away, mind the older folks."

She patted me on the back, wiped her tears and then wiped mine. Then she kind of nudged me very gently toward the door to say good-bye. She did not know when I would be back. I didn't either. But my mother was sick, and she felt I should go to her side.

The woman took me by the hand and slowly led me away. When we were in the street I suddenly broke into tears. As long as we were in James Alley I could see Grandma Josephine waving good-bye to me.

❧ —— ❦

Zahava Stessel (right) *with her sister in Hungary, circa 1937.*

Róza (Rachel) Szász

BY DR. ZAHAVA STESSEL, WRITER

The lace curtains were half-drawn on the large windows facing the quiet street in a Hungarian village. They were untouched for the last twenty-five years. The owner of the house was the elderly Mrs. Schwartz, the last descendent of one of the early settlers.

While she was not highly religious, Mrs. Schwartz often visited the synagogue, ... accompanied by her maid, Boriska, who carried her ivory-covered prayer book.

When the respected Mrs. Schwartz appeared at the entrance wearing her beautiful lace kerchief, people opened a path for her. With carefully measured dignity she reached the first row where she occupied her seat. Then looking up, she nodded slightly to acknowledge the greetings and the warm respect around her. Then, she immersed herself in the reading of *Mirijam,* a Hungarian translation of selected prayers for women.

Later, as the years passed, Mrs. Schwartz limited her visits to the High Holidays and an occasional Saturday. She would wear the same dark blue, silk dress with the white collar on Saturdays, changing to a similar one in black for the Holidays. With her age advancing and her small frame diminishing, the dresses began to reach her ankle, covering the once stylish, dainty, laced shoes. Her steps also became slower, less and less certain, especially when she neared the gate of her home, where she locked herself into a dignified exile.

Noticing Mrs. Schwartz's lonely plight, my grandmother handed me a small package of groceries to take over to her. With the anticipation and the enthusiasm of an eight-year-old entering a mysterious castle, I knocked at the gate. A bit surprised, but with an encouraging smile, the owner herself came to the door. Using a large key, she slowly opened the black iron gate. She led me through the grapevine-covered porch, leading to a summer room with built-in benches and a table.

Asking my name again, Mrs. Schwartz introduced me to Boriska. While she urged me to take a seat next to the table, Boriska headed to the kitchen, from where she emerged with a candy dish. Urged by my hostess, I selected a candy, which I placed in my pocket. Being a bit shy and uneasy with the attention, I politely bade good-bye, leaving the package unmentioned on the bench.

Moved by the experience, I was very quiet at home. Accustomed to providing anonymous assistance, my grand-mother didn't ask details about my visit. By next Friday, how-ever, I was on my way again. This time Boriska was busy cleaning the porch for Saturday, humming an old melody. Meanwhile, her mistress encouraged me to tell her about my friends and my schoolwork.

As our acquaintance grew, the time of my visits extended. I traveled through the memories of Mrs. Schwartz to the beautiful resorts where kings and emperors spent their time. Resting from her chores, Boriska joined us, lis-tening with solemn attention. At times, she was the one who talked about her home in a distant hamlet. Boriska, who was of the Christian faith, left her village at the age of thirteen to serve in two other places before accepting her present position. Here she spent forty-five of her eighty-two years, never married and having lost contact with her family.

Gaining their confidence, I was gradually allowed to see the rest of the home. Except for the master bedroom and Boriska's room, the house was empty. I hardly heard my escort pointing to the locations of the missing piano and the sofa, as she recounted her lost possessions.

The tall, two-door closet in the bedroom remained the inaccessible magical place. My glimpse into the half-empty inside was a short one, as Mrs. Schwartz was taking out the briefcase containing family pictures. Next to it, I envisioned the mythical treasures to be revealed to me one day.

Part of Boriska's story was also reflected in the fading pictures, as her life intertwined with that of her mistress. As was her custom, Boriska waited to comment, until she was asked by her companion, "Do you recall, do you remember?" At times my presence was forgotten, as the ladies re-created the missing segments of their lives. They would then suddenly turn to me apologetically, with kindness toward the child they never had.

It is still unknown to me whether my grandmother ever visited Mrs. Schwartz, but the packages of hope contained larger and larger portions of cooked food. My grandfather's earnest complaints about small servings of meat and other precious commodities at home at a time of war did not deter my grandmother from acts of charity and compassion.

The food was accepted by Mrs. Schwartz always with apology and humility. Even in the days when their movement was exceptionally painful, the two gentle souls occupied their seats at the table, each one urging the other to take more from the preferred delicacy.

The last time I saw Mrs. Schwartz she was sitting on top of a horse-drawn carriage, holding the huge brass key to her gate, as she was taken to the ghetto. With her on the transport, was my grandmother.

While neither one survived the war, the legacy of my grandmother's packages reached beyond the flames of Auschwitz. It created for me memories of benevolence and love to be told to generations of her children and grandchildren.

RESPECT

The old are the precious gem in the center of the household.

—CHINESE PROVERB

※ —— ✦

Rose Kennedy

BY MARIA SHRIVER, JOURNALIST

My grandmother had great style, a quick wit, a snappy sense of humor and a will of steel. She had a tremendous impact on me, not just for what she taught me, but for the way she carried herself.

I remember taking walks with her at Hyannisport. She would walk every day, same time, no matter what. Cars would always drive by, filled with curious tourists asking where the Kennedy compound was. My cousins and I would often give unsuspecting people the wrong directions or tell them we didn't know. My grandmother, on the other hand, would flag people down who appeared lost and ask them what they needed. She would then proceed to introduce herself as the president's mother and invite them for a guided tour of the compound. She felt it was important to always treat people with the utmost respect, the way that she would want to be treated. She would say: "Remember you only have one chance to make an impression and why not make a good one. And last but not least, every one of those people has a vote and you never know when you will need it."

I loved her deeply and miss her every day.

⤳ —— ⤶

Mary Gretzky

BY WAYNE GRETZKY, HOCKEY PLAYER

My grandmother was a tough lady. She loved Frank Mahovlich and all-star wrestling, so you know what I mean. I remember I was playing a game in Brantford once and a guy named Paul Reinhart was checking me. He had me pinned against the boards, right in front of Grandma. There was no glass there. Next thing I know, Grandma was taking her purse and whapping him over the head as hard as she could, yelling, "You leave my boy alone!" Next to Dave Semenko, I'd have taken Grandma any day.

⤳ —— ⤶

I like my drinks strong and my men weak."

–ANN SPILLANE, SOCIAL WORKER
QUOTING HER GRANDMOTHER PEG O'BRIEN

My first feeling on looking at my grandson's face took me aback. It was as if neither of us were present, as if I for a second lost myself and couldn't find him in some ineffable void. No feeling of recognition or of his belonging to me in any way. As I came to, my first articulated feeling was actually one of respect for him.

–ANNE TRUITT, WRITER AND ARTIST

Josephine Baker in 1951.

Elvira MacDonald

Grandmother of Josephine Baker

BY JEANE-CLAUDE BAKER,
SON OF JOSEPHINE BAKER,
AND RESTAURATEUR

I was still a young child when Josephine Baker, the legendary black entertainer of the 1920s, became my second mother. She told me countless stories about her glamorous past as we traveled around the world together. But, oddly, she never spoke about one of the most beloved figures in her life. Years later, while researching what would eventually become *Josephine: The Hungry Heart,* her definitive biography, I learned of Josephine's lifelong devotion to her adoptive grandmother, Elvira MacDonald.

Elvira was born a slave on a tobacco plantation in Holly Springs, Arkansas. In an early autobiography, Josephine had confessed, "A black childhood is always a little sad. . . . My grandmother Elvira often talked about slave days. I adored Grandma. The songs she sang as she rocked me to sleep . . . told of the freedom that would someday come."

Josephine overcame the many obstacles that stood in the path of any ambitious and talented young black woman in the 1920s. She went on to achieve great wealth and inter-national fame—entertaining figures as diverse as de Gaulle, Castro, Princess Grace, and Martin Luther King. Far from the Arkansas plantations of Elvira's youth, Josephine became the mistress of a six-hundred-acre chateau, Les Milandes, in France. She had over twenty gardeners meticulously caring for its sloping lawns and every variety of flower, including the Josephine Rose, a blossom named for her.

At the entrance of the chateau, one always showed off the prize of one's collection. To the astonishment of her neighbors, the entrance to Josephine's chateau was lined with stalks of tobacco—a silent tribute to the grandmother she had never forgotten.

FIVE POEMS FOR GRANDMOTHERS
(excerpt)

III
How little I know
about you finally:

The time you stood
in the nineteenth century
on Yonge Street, a thousand
miles from home, with a brown purse
and a man stole it.

Six children, five who lived.
She never said anything
about those births and the one death;
her mouth closed on a pain
that could neither be told nor ignored.

She used to have such a sense of fun.
Now girls, she would say
when we would tease her.
Her anger though, why
that would curl your hair,
though she never swore.
The worst she could say was:
Don't be foolish.

At eighty she had two teeth pulled out
and walked the four miles home
in the noon sun, placing her feet
in her own hunched shadow.

The bibbed print aprons, the shock
of the red lace dress, the pin
I found at six in your second drawer,
made of white beads, the shape of a star.
What did we ever talk about
but food, health and the weather?

Sons branch out, but
one woman leads to another.
Finally I know you
through your daughters,
my mother, her sisters,
and through myself:

Is this you, this edgy joke
I make, are these your long fingers,
your hair of an untidy bird,
is this your outraged
eye, this grip
that will not give up?

                                        –MARGARET ATWOOD

Rena Bishop

BY CHARLES KURALT,
JOURNALIST

I unbuttoned Eleanor Roosevelt's dress. I was very nervous, though she did her best to make it easy for me.

I had grown up persuaded that Eleanor Roosevelt was the greatest living American, not excluding her husband, the President. This idea came from my grandmother. To her, FDR was a lofty and distant figure, but she felt she knew Mrs. Roosevelt from her column, "My Day," which appeared six days a week in *The Raleigh News and Observer*. My grandmother would walk a mile down the dirt road to the mailbox beside the highway, bring the newspaper home and read to our family at the kitchen table at night. She nearly always read us "My Day." Mrs. Roosevelt frequently expressed her wish for a better life for Americans in those Depression days, a wish my grandmother approved of and shared.

These readings took place by the light of a kerosene lamp. Hardly any farms in our part of North Carolina had electricity in the '30s; the big power companies couldn't see any profit in it. When the light poles of the Rural Electrification Administration finally came marching down that dirt road in 1939 and we got an electric light bulb over the kitchen table, my grandmother gave Mrs. Roosevelt the credit.

Mrs. Roosevelt had been a teacher and thought the country needed better education. My grandmother had been a teacher, too, and thought the same. The middle-aged woman in the White House and the middle-aged housewife on the farm saw eye to eye on everything. They shared a lack of pretension. My grandmother drove her own farm wagon and later her own old Chevrolet; Mrs. Roosevelt took city buses and traveled on trains by ordinary day coach. When Mrs. Roosevelt's memoir, "This Is My Story," appeared in *Ladies' Home Journal* installments, my grandmother saved the magazines in her bookcase where they remained until she died.

So when I finally met Mrs. Roosevelt, it was like meeting a monument. She proved to be a gracious and smiling monument. I was prepared for that. I was not prepared for what followed.

The occasion was Nikita Krushchev's visit to Hyde Park. The radio microphone had just been invented for television use, and as a young reporter for CBS News, I asked Mrs. Roosevelt to wear one so that we could hear the conversation as she showed Krushchev around the house and grounds. She agreed. Then the producer insisted that the apparatus be concealed from the camera's view.

"Mrs. Roosevelt," I said, "I'm going to have to hide the mike inside your dress."

She smiled. "Do whatever you need to do," she said.

I unbuttoned the back of her dress and attached the transmitter to her corset. I passed the microphone cable under her armpit. She obligingly leaned forward and let her dress slide off her shoulders so that I could hook the mike to her bra. As I stood there toying with the underwear of the greatest living American, I wondered what my grandmother would have thought. And I was profoundly grateful to Mrs. Roosevelt for being so matter-of-fact about it all.

Krushchev came and went. The microphone worked fine. When the event was over, Mrs. Roosevelt asked me to drive her down from the main house to her cottage, Val-Kill, and invited me in for tea.

"But you'll have to excuse me for half an hour," she said. "I must do my daily bit of writing now. I write a newspaper column, you know."

"Yes," I said. "I know."

I blurted out the story of my grandmother's kitchen-table readings of "My Day" and said something about my grandmother's career as a rural teacher.

Mrs. Roosevelt said, "Your grandmother sounds like just the sort of person we need more of."

I was able to give a heartfelt reply. I said, "She felt the same about you."

Grandchildren are the dots that connect the lines from generation to generation.

–LOIS WYSE, WRITER

Angie Miller Williams with her
granddaughter Lucinda Williams in 1975.

Angie Miller Williams

BY LUCINDA WILLIAMS, MUSICIAN,
SINGER, AND SONGWRITER

My paternal grandmother, Angie Miller Williams
(Mimma to all of us), was a woman of remarkable
wisdom, courage, and good humor. She taught me patience,
tolerance for the ways of others, the importance of simple
honesty, and how to laugh when there isn't a lot to laugh
about.

When she was almost eighty and wearing a black arm-band in observation of the moratorium against the Vietnam War, a grocery store checkout clerk who knew her slightly asked her if someone in the family had died.

"Oh, mercy, yes," she answered, "Thousands and thousands of them."

She died turning a hundred. I miss her.

❧ —— ❧

Grandma Page

BY DAN RATHER, JOURNALIST

Grandma Page was a big woman of unsurpassed energy. Energy–but not electricity. There was no electricity on the Page family farm.

My maternal grandmother was up at three-thirty or four o'clock in the morning to bake and churn and get ready for the cotton fields. At night, after the cooking and sewing, there was energy left for her reading.

I doubt that Grandma Page went beyond the sixth grade in school, and hers was not a home filled with books, yet Grandma revered reading.

"Come, Danny, I'll read to you," she would say. That was enough to make me come running. It meant story time, and story time most often was Bible time. The Bible was quite literally an open book for our family. An open Bible meant that the good book was alive and well and had been lately in use.

Grandma Page knew all of my favorite Bible stories and catered to my taste for the great deeds it recorded, especially those of Joshua at the Battle of Jericho. Meaning no disrespect to Grandmother's religious beliefs, I should clarify here that her Bible offerings were meant less to serve the cause of piety than to serve our need for entertainment. Joshua was my Sylvester Stallone, I guess. She had no radio, wouldn't even hear the word "television" for another decade, so we had to reach out for pretty simple forms of fun in Bloomington, Texas.

I am told that I was the first of the Pages or Rathers to make it through college. I've often thought of those evenings when Grandma Page read me Bible stories by the light of a coal-oil lamp in her little house in the Texas cotton fields. She showed me that books were filled with dreams and excitement, faith and wisdom: my education began as I sat in her lap, embraced between Grandma and the Bible. Now that I am older, I suspect she may have been, in her way, even more heroic than Joshua.

LINEAGE

My grandmothers were strong.
They followed plows and bent to toil.
They moved through fields sowing seed.
They touched earth and grain grew.

They were full of sturdiness and singing.
My grandmothers were strong.

My grandmothers are full of memories
Smelling of soap and onions and wet clay
With veins rolling roughly over quick hands
They have many clean words to say.
My grandmothers were strong.
Why am I not as they?

—Margaret Walker

Patsy Hughes Irvine

COLLECTIBLES SPECIALIST
AND GRANDMOTHER

in her own words

I've always loved professional wrestling, but I didn't become "The Wrestling Grandma" until about nine years ago. We went to see Bret Hart at the Cow Palace in San Francisco. My husband, my daughter, grandkids Jennifer and Katie, and I had our usual front-row seats. The match was getting ready to begin, and Bret spotted me and shouted, "Hi, Grandma!" "You know it!" I yelled back. A bunch of kids in the audience looked over at me and stared. "Hey, you're Bret Hart's grandma?!" they said. I just smiled.

Well, pretty soon it was all over the Cow Palace that Bret Hart's grandma was sitting up front. It became a thing. And I'm hard to miss. I wear the same silver-sequined jacket to every match. A friend of mine had said to me before this all began, "You can't go to the wrestling matches dressed like everybody else! I have the perfect jacket for you." And she did. Under those stadium lights the sequins flash and shine like crazy. They look like diamonds. My husband and I would go to the matches whenever the WWF came to the Cow Palace, every three months or so. Soon kids started coming up to me asking me to sign their tickets,

Patsy H. Irvine, "The Wrestling Grandma," and Sycho Sid at
the Cow Palace, San Francisco, July 25, 1996.

programs, or wrestling cards. So, I signed them "The Wrestling Grandma."

Oh, we used to be so trashy. The family would wait till
the stadium lights dimmed and the matches were about to
start, and then we'd make our entrance. Well, I would,
anyway. Father is very sedate, but I would go strutting in
with my silver-sequined jacket sparkling. The crowd would
yell, "The Wrestling Grandma's here! Let the games begin!!"
The wrestlers usually greet me, too, shouting from the stage
something like, "Hey grandma, cross your fingers for me!"

When my granddaughter, Katie, was just five weeks old we took her to a Hulk Hogan match. We dressed her in a red T-shirt that said "The Hulk Rules" with a matching headband and yellow diapers. The Hulk loved it. He cradled her in his arms and brought her on stage with him. There was Katie, sleeping like an angel. A few years later, when she was three, we went to see Hulk again. During the fight, he fell over the ropes right in front of her and lay still. Katie ran over to him and said, "Hulk, get up! Hulk, get up!" Hulk, not wanting her to worry, opened one eye and whispered, "Katie, I'm just taking a rest." "Oh, okay," she said, and walked away. After the matches, we always go back home, make hot fudge sundaes, and talk about the matches and all that jazz. It's a family thing. And we all have a great time.

⊸———⊹

A ll the world is a stage."

–BIG BIRD, ADVICE FROM
HIS GRANDMOTHER, GRANNY BIRD

⊸———⊹

N o matter what they say, no matter what they do to you, you just go on out there and be the best you can be. Listen hard when you're on stage. That's me you'll hear clapping."

–VICKY PHILLIPS, WRITER
QUOTING HER GRANDMOTHER ANABELLE ENGLAND

∽∶ —— ∶∾

Anna Lesizza

BY CATHRYN GIRARD,
FOUNDER AND PRESIDENT,
CARING GRANDPARENTS OF AMERICA

W hen she was sixteen years old, my Grandmother Lesizza came to the United States by boat, alone.

She came from what is now Czechoslovakia or the Czech Republic and could not read or write when she came to America. She had an aunt who had previously immigrated to the United States. She had only the promise of one familiar face on the other side of the Atlantic. Grampa Lesizza had also come to America from Czechoslovakia when he was young. He left Europe through an Italian port. Because, like my grandmother, he could neither read nor write at the time, he could not correct the Italian Customs

Official when he misspelled his Czech name "Lesizza." So, Lesizza it remained.

One afternoon, the adults were playing a very simple guessing game in which one person gives the initials of a celebrity. Everyone has to figure out who the initials represent by asking questions. Gramma Lesizza presented the initials "V.H." to the questioners who determined that the mysterious "V.H." was a male movie star. Beyond this point, however, they were stumped. Eventually, everyone gave up in total frustration. With a triumphant smile, Gramma Lesizza announced, "Villiam Holden!" There was a collective groan and a chorus of "Ma, it's William Holden!" In spite of this information Gramma Lesizza remained somewhat indignant. The spunk and courage that brought her thousands of miles across the ocean to her new home remained firmly intact throughout her long life.

It wasn't until I was in my thirties that I discovered just how much I'd become my grandmother's granddaughter. I wasn't cowed by situations that made others slink into a corner or give up. I made many unconventional choices, like going to law school at the age of forty. My sisters and I were the third generation of a strong matriarchal line. Today, I often think of Gramma Lesizza. I silently thank her for her strength, for her courage. Many days I need them.

Grandmother's Table

ADAPTED FROM THE BROTHERS GRIMM

Once there was a feeble old woman whose husband died and left her all alone, so she went to live with her son and his wife and their own little daughter. Every day the old woman's sight dimmed and her hearing grew worse, and sometimes at dinner her hands trembled so badly the peas rolled off her spoon or the soup ran from her cup. The son and his wife could not help but be annoyed at the way she spilled her meal all over the table, and one day, after she knocked over a glass of milk, they told each other enough was enough.

They set up a small table for her in the corner next to the broom closet and made the old woman eat her meals there. She sat all alone, looking with tear-filled eyes across the room at the others. Sometimes they spoke to her while they ate, but usually it was to scold her for dropping a bowl or a fork.

One evening just before dinner, the little girl was busy playing on the floor with her building blocks, and her father asked her what she was making. "I'm building a little table for you and mother," she smiled, "so you can eat by yourselves in the corner someday when I get big."

Her parents sat staring at her for some time and then suddenly both began to cry. That night they led the old woman back to her place at the big table. From then on she ate with the rest of the family, and her son and his wife never seemed to mind a bit when she spilled something every now and then.

–ADAPTED BY WILLIAM BENNETT,
THE BOOK OF VIRTUES

❧ —— ❧

The women said to Naomi, "Praise the Lord! He has given you a grandson today to take care of you. . . . Your daughter-in-law loves you. And now she has given you a grandson, who will bring new life to you and give you security in your old age." Naomi took the child, held him close, and took care of him.

–RUTH 4:14–16

❧ —— ❧

For every fish in the sea, there's a dozen crabs crawling the earth."

–KEVIN MARRINAN, WRITER
ADVICE FROM HIS GRANDMOTHER

MaMaw, my paternal grandmother, said, "Baby, a woman carries a Kleenex, but a lady carries a handkerchief." When she died at eighty-nine, we buried this lady with a handkerchief in her hands.

–MICHAEL E. BONNER, WRITER
ON HIS GRANDMOTHER MAMAW BONNER

❧ —— ❧

Don't go acting like the Queen of Sheba–because you're not."

–VICKY PHILLIPS, AUTHOR
ADVICE FROM HER GRANDMOTHER

❧ —— ❧

Emma Haines

BY ERMA BOMBECK, WRITER (1927–1996)

We had an understanding Grandma and I. She didn't treat me like a child and I didn't treat her like a mother. We played the game by the rules. If I didn't slam her doors and sass, then she didn't spank and lecture me.

Yetta

BY FRAN DRESCHER, ACTRESS

Ann Guilbert, who made her first appearance as Yetta in the second episode [of the CBS hit television series *The Nanny*], has since become a more permanent fixture, loved by everyone. The first time she was on the show, *my* grandmother (the real Yetta) was quite insulted.

"Why'd ya have to put her in a home? I don't live in a home, I got my own apartment!" she said as she flipped her Bic and took a long drag off her cigarette.

It didn't matter to her that the character would get bigger laughs if we made her a little forgetful. Nothing mattered until that day she desperately needed a last-minute appointment at the beauty parlor (on a Saturday, yet) and got in on account of she's *Yetta,* "the Nanny's" grandma! As her personal fame and glory rose in the neighborhood with each appearance by Ann Guilbert on the show, so did Yetta's appreciation for her counterpart.

*Michael Dorris (far right) with his grandmother Laura Hamilton
at the Governor's Writing Awards.*

Laura Hamilton

BY MICHAEL DORRIS (1945–1997),
AUTHOR OF CLOUD CHAMBER

For ninety-six of my grandmother's ninety-seven (and counting) years, she lived under her own roof–first on a mint farm on an Idaho panhandle reservation, then in various houses in Tacoma which she shared, over time, with first one then a second husband and three sons, before settling into being mostly alone.

An avid and cut-throat card player, as the population surrounding her diminished, my grandmother shifted her primary game from bridge to pinochle to cribbage to, finally, as she called it, "solitary." Still and all, a worn (and marked) deck always reposed squarely in its place of honor in the center of her kitchen table, waiting for an easy mark to sit down and take up the challenge.

In my memory, my grandmother has never been what you'd call "easy." Five years ago when I took her as my date to the Governor's Writing Awards ceremony in Olympia (she wore what could only be termed a prom dress), the then chief executive of the state of Washington, spying what he believed to be a sweet little old lady, leaned over patronizingly and shouted, "Welcome to the capitol."

"I was a registered nurse for fifty years," my grandmother replied in an ascending tone of voice. "I was working at the hospital where you were born, and YOU WERE A BAD BABY. Drove your mother crazy with your whining."

End of conversation.

Even with a person as tough as my grandmother, however, time eventually takes its toll. With fading eyesight and selectively bad hearing (she always seems to hear what she wants to know and tunes out the rest), my grandmother finally, last August, consented to move into a retirement home apartment in her old neighborhood. It's an excellent facility, and the space allows a resident to be surrounded with her own belongings, cook her own meals, have as much privacy as she wants—while still having access to medical and other kinds of assistance should it become necessary.

Nevertheless, it was with some trepidation that I paid my first visit to the new digs last Labor Day weekend. How would my grandmother adjust to the change? How would I find her?

The first clue was set in its accustomed spot on the familiar kitchen table. As I pulled up a chair, my grandmother automatically began to shuffle.

"So Grandma," I asked. "How do you like it here?"

"Michael," she said, her voice strong and full of enthusiasm, "it's wonderful. These old folks can't play cards worth a damn and I'm making a fortune."

ANSWERS

I f you listen to advice and are willing to learn, one day you will be wise.

–PROVERBS 19:20

Mary Hall

BY DIANE KEATON,
ACTRESS AND DIRECTOR

M y grandmother once said, "I don't know that there's a heaven. Nobody ever lit a match and said, 'Here's heaven. Walk right in.'"

ANSWERS

If I envy anyone it must be
My grandmother in a long ago
Green summer, who hurried
Between kitchen and orchard on small
Uneducated feet, and took easily
All shining fruits into her eager hands.

That summer I hurried too, wakened
To books and music and circling philosophies.
I sat in the kitchen sorting through volumes of answers
That could not solve the mystery of the trees.

My grandmother stood among her kettles and ladles.
Smiling, in faulty grammar,
She praised my fortune and urged my lofty career.
So to please her I studied—but I will remember always
How she poured confusion out, how she cooled and labeled
All the wild sauces of the brimming year.

—MARY OLIVER

Rosa Murray

BY FORMER FIRST LADY
ROSALYNN CARTER

My grandmother, who lived on a farm, had a large vegetable garden right beside her house. In it she would have one long row of flowers. When we visited her she always wanted us to help gather the vegetables, and when we got tired, she would say, "Don't think about it, just look at the flowers."

My grandmother taught me to look for beauty in any kind of situation I find myself in.

My grandmother] lived by herself on top of a mountain in the Sierra Nevadas. Her philosophy was, "If you're afraid of dying, you're afraid to live."

–CLINT EASTWOOD, ACTOR AND DIRECTOR
ON HIS GRANDMOTHER VIRGINIA MCLANAHAN RUNNER

Dorothy Grega

BY TOMMY HILFIGER, DESIGNER

My grandmother always gave me the best advice throughout her life, and it seems she was never wrong. Whenever I struggled with a decision or direction to take, she would say, without fail, "There are two roads you may take in life, the low road or the high road. It's up to you to choose how you want to get there." In my life, I've chosen to take the higher of the two, which was not always the easiest way, but in the end the best one. In turn, I've advised my children of the same. Nana, I thank you.

My grandmother Rose gave me wonderful advice about men, "Be more patient and wear shorter skirts."

–*OLIVIA GOLDSMITH, WRITER*
ON HER GRANDMOTHER ROSE JACOBS

A hard head makes for a sore ass." No truer words ever came from false teeth.

–WILLIE NELSON, MUSICIAN
ON HIS GRANDMOTHER "MAMA" NELSON

⟶

Antonia Baldo Perez

BY JOSE VIVES, ELEVATOR OPERATOR

My grandmother, Antonia Baldo Perez, was a woman ahead of her time. She was raised in Cuba in the late nineteenth century. An early suffragist, she was arrested several times while fighting for women's rights in her homeland. She was a joyous, lively woman and a wonderful storyteller. She never let me or my brothers and sister call her grandma. "My name is Antonia," she'd say. "Call me Antonia." In 1932, shortly after I was born, the political situation in Cuba worsened and my family left. We moved to a beautiful seaside village in Spain called Benidorm. The summer of 1942, ten years after we arrived, will always hold a special place in my memory. That summer my grandmother taught me a lesson I will never forget.

It was shortly after the Spanish Civil War and food was scarce. One day, while in a local fish store I spotted a lovely piece of fish. Knowing my family did not have enough money to buy the fish, I took it. At the time, I thought I was helping my grandmother by providing her and my family with something they needed. But it didn't belong to me and I got caught. When my grandmother found out it seemed the whole world had come to an end! I was her favorite grandchild. She was so ashamed of my behavior, so disappointed in me. She was going to make sure that the punishment fit the crime.

My grandmother knew, perhaps better than anyone, how much I loved the ocean. I have had a lifelong romance with the sea. But for the summer of 1942, I would not set eyes on it again. While my three brothers and sister swam and splashed in the water and played in the sand, I had to stay inside my grandmother's cottage. It was a long summer and it was a big lesson for me.

To raise a child, you need to give both discipline and love. Antonia gave both. Everything I needed to learn about raising children I learned from my grandmother.

Lillie Lulkin

"Advice from My Grandmother" (excerpt)
BY ALICE HOFFMAN, WRITER

Between men and women, love is not only blind but stupid. Oh, sure, love has a sense of humor, but the punch line is usually sex, money, despair, or kids, and none of these are particularly funny. Here's how you test if love is real. Broil a chicken (with a side dish of potatoes, naturally) and invite him over. Cook badly. Even if you're already a bad cook, make it worse. Trust me, it's easy. Throw in anything you want. Too much salt, too much pepper. Feed him and see what he says. A complaint means he's thinking about himself, and always will. A compliment means he'll never make a living. But a man who says, "Let's go to a restaurant," now he's a real man. Order expensive, and see what he's got to say then. Kiss him good-night. Go ahead, don't be afraid. Do you hear your blood in your head moving too fast? Are you faint? Do you need a Tylenol? Are you sick to your stomach and shaky in your knees? That's love all right, so don't fight it, honey, because in such matters, no human is immune. Not even you.

Dorothy L. Guistra

BY CAPTAIN SCOTT O'GRADY, U.S. AIR FORCE

The thing I admire most about Nana is her zest for life. To her, life is a celebration. From her "Dear Abby" clippings around the kitchen and her water aerobics, to her deep faith in God, she is an inspiration to me. She has taught me that you need to live life to its fullest, because you never know what tomorrow is going to bring.

When I returned from Bosnia, Nana was waiting with an American flag in one hand and a bottle of champagne in the other, cheering my safe return. During our drive to the White House, Nana insisted that she was going to be speechless while we visited with President and Mrs. Clinton. None of us believed her–Nana has *never* been speechless. The minute she saw them, she ran to shake the president's hand and began talking his ear off with her stories. Later, the president commented on how impressed he was with my grandmother. I, too, am impressed with Nana. She is a ray of sunshine to everyone with whom she comes in contact. I hope I have as much energy and life as she does when I am her age.

ADVICE FROM NANA

Always wear your clothes like they have only been yours.
And never pay retail unless it's divine.
Eat only what you want on your plate and leave anything.
Eat dessert and hors d'oeuvres and skip the entrees, just
*   enjoy.*
Make men buy you presents, and if you don't like their taste,
teach them what you love.
If you can't teach them what you love, leave them.
And darling, don't pick your split ends.
Look into the eyes of the person you are talking to,
and they will believe you.
If you want to stop someone from criticizing you,
let your chin quiver just a bit, eyes fill up, yes,
there that's it.

Don't stand in the corner at a party, walk over to the books
and enjoy them, because at least that's fun
and you should never be uncomfortable at a party. God
*   forbid,*
you are so gorgeous.
Remember I love you.
Remember to call me and tell me everything.
Remember this pearl necklace is yours, and the china.
Don't sit with your legs apart,
you're sure to get the wrong boyfriends that way, I surely
*   did.*

I had to be told a hundred times too.
Did I tell you I love you?
Lord, you look like your mother at that age,
and she was a wild one.
I had my hands full with her, at least you got her brains.
Thank God for that, she was a whiz.

Now remember, if someone asks your name
more than three times,
Forget them! Don't tell them!
I never would and I met everyone I needed to.
When you want to know a good restaurant in a strange
*   town,*
don't ask at the hotel, just walk a bit, read the menus,
and smell the air when you walk in.
You can always tell by the smell.
And Darling, even a good man can be picked that way . . .
I always found good men by their smell.

–JUDYTH HILL

Annie Henderson

BY MAYA ANGELOU, AUTHOR OF I KNOW WHY THE CAGED BIRD SINGS

When my grandmother was raising me in Stamps, Arkansas, she had a particular routine when people who were known to be whiners entered her store. Whenever she saw a known complainer coming, she would call me from whatever I was doing and say conspiratorially, "Sister, come inside. Come." Of course I would obey.

My grandmother would ask the customer, "How are you doing today, Brother Thomas?" And the person would reply, "Not so good." There would be a distinct whine in the voice. "Not so good today, Sister Henderson. You see, it's this summer. It's this summer heat. I just hate it. Oh, I hate it so much. It just frazzles me up and frazzles me down. I just hate the heat. It's almost killing me." Then my grandmother would stand stoically, her arms folded, and mumble, "Uh-huh, uh-huh." And she would cut her eyes at me to make certain that I had heard the lamentation.

At another time a whiner would mewl, "I hate plowing. That packed-down dirt ain't got no reasoning, and mules ain't got good sense . . . Sure ain't. It's killing me. I can't ever seem to get done. My feet and my hands stay sore, and I get dirt in my eyes and up my nose. I just can't stand it." And my grand-mother, again stoically with her arms folded, would say, "Uh-huh, uh-huh," and then look at me and nod.

As soon as the complainer was out of the store, my grandmother would call me to stand in front of her. And then she would say the same thing she said at least a thou-sand times, it seemed to me, "Sister, did you hear what Brother So-and-So or Sister Much to Do complained about? You heard that?" And I would nod. Mamma would continue, "Sister, there are people who went to sleep all over the world last night, poor and rich and white and black, but they will never wake again. Sister, those who expected to rise did not, their beds became their cooling boards and their blan-kets became their winding sheets. And those dead folks would give anything, anything at all for just five minutes of this weather or ten minutes of that plowing that person was grumbling about. So watch yourself about complaining, Sister. What you're supposed to do when you don't like a thing is change it. If you can't change it, change the way you think about it. Don't complain."

It is said that persons have few teachable moments in their lives. Mamma seemed to have caught me at each one I had between the age of three and thirteen. Whining is not only graceless, but can be dangerous. It can alert a brute that a victim is in the neighborhood.

The lightbulb in the bathroom was blazing a white star in the mirror, and looking at it, I was surprised by how much pleasure and agony could burst from one's heart at the same time. For once, I understood what my grandma used to say about happiness. She'd say that it came from breathing air that escaped from a tiny hole in heaven. But if you breathed too much of it, you became sick with the desire to go there, and you couldn't live your life properly.

–VICTOR MARTINEZ, PARROT IN THE OVEN

—❧ —— ❧—

My paternal grandmother, who was Lebanese, used to say that "the reason men sweat so much when they sleep is that all their pent-up, choked-back tears come out at night."

–MARLO THOMAS, ACTRESS
ON HER GRANDMOTHER MARGARET THOMAS

—❧ —— ❧—

Never forget: Men begin as little boys. They go through a spell of playing at being grown-up, but in the end, they remain little boys."

–DEBBIE KESLING, WRITER
ADVICE FROM HER GRANDMOTHER LOLA MARTIN

Dubba Markova

DAWNA MARKOVA, WRITER

Once my grandmother pointed at a fat man who stepped out of a gleaming black Buick wearing a raccoon coat. I said he was rich. "Look with your other eyes. Look into his heart. Do you see there is no light there?" I must have nodded, because she whispered in a dry voice, "He is a very poor man. A young soul perhaps. Now look over there."

She pointed to a small boy wearing a red striped polo shirt who had no legs and wheeled himself down the street on a makeshift board with roller skate wheels. I had seen him many times before, laughing, whistling, joking with the women who leaned out windows to hang their laundry on the lines that stretched from one building to the next.

"But Grandma, that poor boy has no legs!"

"*Ketzaleh*, try something for me. Slip him over your mind as if he were a sweater you were putting on. Feel what it's like to be him. Feel his heart. Now look at him again, look at that heart. It's pure gold and wide as the sky. He's a rich old soul whose path is to teach all of us about joy!"

Don't sigh too often, you'll blow your good luck away!"

—CAROLINE LIN, MENTAL HEALTH WORKER
ADVICE FROM HER GRANDMOTHER, LUI SU RU

✧ —— ✧

Mary Connerty

BY MARIANNE CAMPBELL,
PHOTOGRAPHY AGENT

Three months prior to my Nana's death, she was diag-
nosed with another cancer-related ailment. My mother
was consoling her and offered to say a few prayers including
one to my Nana's long deceased husband. In response, my
Nana told my mother the story of her friend Rosalie who
had recently been driven to a doctor's appointment by her
husband. In a freak accident, Rosalie's coat got caught in the
car door and she was dragged by the automobile and killed.

"What's the point?" my mother asked.

My Nana's reply was, "Take a cab and leave the hus-
bands out of it."

✧ —— ✧

Mattie Carter

BY NINA CARTER KING,
EDUCATIONAL CONSULTANT

I once asked my grandmother why she didn't cry at funerals. She replied, "God allows people to come into our lives on borrowed time. It's like a friend lending you a sweater. You never know when that friend will ask for the sweater back. And when he or she does, you'll have to return it. The sweater doesn't belong to you and neither do the people in your life. God only lends them to us on borrowed time for a special reason."

❧ —— ❧

Margie "Nanny" Ward

BY GARRY MARSHALL, DIRECTOR

My Grandma was blind so she used to make me read books aloud to her. She taught me that it didn't matter if you could see the words on the page. As long as you understood them you could enjoy them. And I've been enjoying words ever since.

Naomi and Wynonna Judd with Pauline Judd Rideout (center).

Pauline Judd Rideout

BY WYNONNA JUDD,
SINGER, SONGWRITER, AND MUSICIAN

My grandmother used to say, "Wash your hands and say your prayers because germs and Jesus are invisible but they're everywhere!"

Mary Stevens Rhinelander

BY EDITH WHARTON (1862–1937),
AUTHOR OF THE AGE OF INNOCENCE

During one of our Paris winters my dear old grandmother, my mother's mother, paid us a long visit. . . . I
always recall her seated in an arm-chair, her undimmed eyes
bent over some exquisitely fine needlework. I hope she
sometimes went for a walk or a drive, and enjoyed a few
glimpses of grown-up society; but for me she exists only as
a motionless and gently smiling figure, whose one gesture
was to lay aside her stitching for her ear-trumpet at my
approach. When she was with us I was constantly in her
room; and my way of returning her affection was to read
aloud to her.

I had just discovered a volume of Tennyson among my
father's books, and for hours I used to shout the "Idyls of the
King" and "The Lord of Burleigh" through the trumpet of my
long-suffering ancestress. Not being more than six or seven
years old I understood hardly anything of what I was
reading, or rather I understood it in my own way, which was
most often not the poet's; as in the line from "The Lord of
Burleigh", "and he made a loving consort", where I read *concert* for consort, and concluded (being already addicted to
rash generalizations) that a gentleman's first act after mar-

riage was to give his spouse a concert, in gratitude for which "a faithful wife was she."

I suspect no one else in the house could bear to be read aloud to by me, for I do not remember attempting it on any one but my grandmother.

Never let anyone who comes to you leave unless they are a little happier for having been with you."

–DEE SHEPHERD
QUOTING HER GRANDMOTHER
PAULINE "BABA" NAVLAN

*Ina Macmillan Bigelow holding
her granddaughter Esther, circa 1935.*

Ina Macmillan Bigelow

BY ESTHER MACMILLAN
BIGELOW GATES, EDUCATOR

Ina Macmillan Bigelow was born in the late 1800s in Char-lottetown, Prince Edward Island. After working as a school-teacher in Canada she got a job at the Perkins Institute for the

Blind in Boston and left for America. At the Perkins Institute she met a young student named Edward Bigelow. Edward was a charismatic and intelligent man who had been blinded in early childhood as the result of a riding accident. Teacher and student were soon quite taken with one another. Much to the chagrin of their parents and the Perkins Institute, which strictly forbade fraternization between teachers and students, Edward and Ina fell in love. When, despite the young couple's devotion to one another, their familes remained vehemently opposed to the relationship, they ran away together to Canada. They were married in New Brunswick and eventually settled in Norwood, Rhode Island. They had two sons, Bruce and Gordon, my father. Edward supported his family by tuning pianos and raising chickens. Money was tight and life was not easy, but the family was never short on love or support. Ina taught her sons to follow their hearts and their dreams, just as she had. And both did. On the strength of their hard work and ambition, they received full scholarships to Brown University. Both young men brought bagged lunches to class, being unable to afford to buy lunch with the other students, but they graduated Phi Beta Kappa and then went on to receive doctorates. My father became a minister, and his brother vice president of his alma mater.

I remember fondly visiting my grandparents in Rhode Island. To watch my grandfather around the farm, you would never suspect he was blind. He moved effortlessly and expertly around the property, going about his chores, feeding chickens, pumping water from the well. He had an old player piano with countless rolls of music. In my memory, Grandma's kitchen was perpetually filled with the warm rich smell of peanut-butter cookies. She always had a plate on the table waiting for her grandchildren. I later learned that every visit, my grandmother took money from the sugar bowl where she stored it and discreetly pressed it into my mother's hand. Though she and my grandfather were just getting by themselves, there was always something to spare for her children and grandchildren. She is a woman whose heart and dreams governed her life. In doing so, she did not find wealth, but she always found happiness. I recently came upon an old letter that she had written to my father. In it she said,

> *Thank you for your beautiful thoughts and words on Mother's Day. But truly, every day is Mother's Day for me because of my children and grandchildren.*

My grandmother's is a legacy of love that has stayed with me always and will be passed on for generations to come.

Always remember, no matter what you become, that you put your pants on one leg at a time just like everybody else."

–MATT LEBLANC, ACTOR
ADVICE FROM HIS GRANDMOTHER

Berthe Pinto with her mother, Gabrielle Tilche,
and daughter Nora Pinto in Cairo, 1934.

Rebecca Alhadeff and Berthe Pinto

BY GINI ALHADEFF,
AUTHOR OF THE SUN AT MIDDAY:
TALES OF A MEDITERRANEAN FAMILY

Grandmothers are dangerous vehicles of propaganda because they appear harmless. They are the first living antiquities in one's life. I had two of them when I was born in a land of antiquities, Egypt. One was an Alexandrian through and through: she had an Italian passport, spoke lame Italian, kitchen Arabic, perfect French and English, but all with a foreign accent. The other was born in Izmir and was swept off by my grandfather to Rhodes where they lived till Mussolini's racial laws were passed and they left for Alexandria so their children could go to school.

I saw them both as ancient and staid. The Turkish grandmother took me to the Sporting Club in her Austin, whose interior was upholstered in fragrant chocolate-brown leather. Sitting next to her on the back seat, I tilted my head back to look through the half-moon–shaped window as it filled with cascades of crimson bougainvillea tumbling over the gates of the club. There, one day, a lady walked over to my grandmother and observed dryly that she didn't think her dress suited her at all. My aunt was irate, but my grandmother said placidly, "Poor woman, when she gets home she'll so regret her unkindness."

Her idea of dieting was to go to Montecatini to drink the waters and eat tortellini to make the water palatable: she invariably gained twenty pounds every time she went.

The Alexandrian grandmother thought you had to live hidden to live happy, and she embroidered her life away. I remember thinking it was a painstaking way to spend one's time, separating a thin silk thread from a spool, weaving it through a needle, then endlessly affixing one stitch next to another in an uneven pattern that is called "the painted stitch" till an entire flower petal was filled in. She embroidered cushions and by the end of her life had completed more than a hundred of them. The designs were taken from Turkish motifs: squarish flowers with leaves and stems twisting around them in geometric precision. She never discussed what she was doing; she simply embroidered modestly, methodically.

There was no pretense at a career or at making art; it was simply an occupation. She listened to the radio and embroidered, her glasses on her nose, her hair squashed beneath a transparent net. She couldn't care less what she wore; she gave up on vanity the day her son died in a car accident. She wore gray and sometimes lilac, her favorite color, which, in Italy, the country where she ended her days, is a color of mourning.

I did not want to be influenced by either the Turkish grandmother or the Alexandrian–their lives seemed dull to me. Ever since I can remember, I wanted the life of the men in my family, of the men I saw around me. When I finally got around to trying the "painted stitch" just a few months ago, it was in the spirit of traveling to distant lands, the way certain women like Freya Stark or Isabelle Eberhardt many decades ago had ventured into the deserts of Arabia, or into the world of men.

I found that embroidering is more exotic than going to the moon: diligent, tedious repetition takes one right into a trance, from trance to thoughtless thought, and from that to a certain modest and immodest clarity. There was a great deal that my handy and crafty grandmother must have understood from her thousand sessions with needle and thread and the limitless sky. I learned from her without knowing that I did so, thinking I would escape "womanishness" before understanding the freedom it brings. Beware of grandmothers who teach what cannot be untaught: You'll know them by the dullness of their ways.

Zerlina Dickerman in 1935.

Zerlina Katz Dickerman

BY LAURA DICKERMAN,
TEACHER AND WRITER

My grandmother is the ultimate romantic. Even her name, Zerlina, has romantic origins. She was named after her grandmother, who was named after the character in

Mozart's opera *Don Giovanni*. Zerlina Katz Dickerman has shaped my view of love, and set the highest standard possible. Grandma believes in love at first sight: in sudden, lightning, 100-percent-sure love. Whenever I have a boyfriend, she asks, "Is he the one?" If I say I'm not sure, she says, "Well, then he isn't!" She should know.

Grandma came from a wealthy family who lived in the grand old hotels on the Upper West Side in New York City. They stayed in each hotel for maybe a year or so at a time. They called room service every night and had clean sheets every morning. When she was eighteen years old, Grandma made a white bathing suit in sewing class and needed a white pair of pumps to model it. She hated to shop, so she sent her mother, who found the "nicest" shoe salesman in a shoe store down on Union Square. After the show, my grandmother returned the shoes and the young shoe salesman asked her out on a date. She said fine, "because there was something about him" . . . but it had to be an early date because an older man was picking her up in his limo for a late theater date. Well, Grandpa wouldn't leave, so she had to cancel her second date. They eloped because her parents didn't approve. She wore a pink raw silk dress; it's still in her closet.

When Grandma and Grandpa first moved into their little apartment, Grandma tried hard to be the perfect wife. She cooked a chicken forgetting to remove the plastic bag of innards. Later, she became a gourmet cook: "Cooking for someone is one of the best ways to express your love for them."

They didn't have much furniture in the early days, and their living room was empty except for a badminton net. When Grandpa got home from work they would play badminton, and Grandma wore a silk teddy. They were so in love with each other.

Since Grandpa died ten years ago, she is not the woman she was. She tells me that she misses him every single day. But that has not kept Grandma from life. And she doesn't fear death. Her eyes are bright blue, her hair silver, her breasts heavy, and her fingers stained from years of nicotine. She can eat a spoonful of wasabi or hot chili oil and never blink. She loves a cold vodka, straight up, no fruit to spoil the symmetry. She speaks her mind. She loves a good dirty joke but she can never retell it successfully. She is an artist. She still gets the giggles. She visits my parents in Vermont and goes fishing in a wide-brimmed straw hat. She can catch a lake trout, clean it, bone it, and cook it with a delicious mustard sauce. She takes me out to dinner once a week. I can tell Grandma anything. I think about her and Grandpa, about sudden, lightning, 100-percent-sure love. I ask her for some words of advice. Grandma says, "Where there's a will . . . there's a relative." Or, "Don't cut chicken on a wooden platter."

Though this is not what I'd had in mind, I've lived for thirty-three years with her as my grandmother so I've learned about love. I learn not to compromise, not to settle. I learn to believe in romance, in unconditional love. I learn that she feeds me love with pear tarts and potato gratin and

Zerlina Dickerman in 1996.

stuffed broiled lobsters and extra horseradish in the cocktail sauce.

I also learn that I have nothing to fear from growing older, as long as I can do it with the grace, humor, and style that Zerlina Katz Dickerman, age eighty-one, does.

Mary Wittenberg

BY SHARI GELLER,
AUTHOR OF FATAL CONVICTIONS,
AND HER SEVEN-YEAR-OLD SON, JOSH

I asked my son what he learned from his surrogate grand-mother Mary, and he told me: "Look fast, think fast, but don't move fast." I asked him what that meant, and he referred to a story she once told him about spotting a road-runner when she went to Arizona. She ran to get her camera to take a picture of it for him. When she returned the road-runner was gone. My son decided the lesson was to stay put and just enjoy what you see because if you run to capture it, it'll be gone. But then, my son is a philosopher at heart.

Mattie Gossage

BY ALANA STEWART,
MODEL AND ACTRESS

My grandmother was the central force in my life. My mother left me with her when I was one and a half years old, and I lived with her on and off over the years. She's the one that instilled in me the values that I have today. She was a strict, God-fearing, Southern Baptist woman who used to tell me, "You shouldn't kiss a boy until you are engaged." Obviously, that was one piece of advice I never followed.

You're not going to die," I tell Grandma. "Don't even think that way."

"Let's dance." Grandma gets up from the table and sticks out her arms, her wrists limp, waiting in the air for me to bow and ask for her company, be the gentleman caller.

Grandma and I begin to dance in the middle aisle of Denny's restaurant to the loud bop music.

"Isn't this chic?"

After one song in Denny's I escort her next door to the dance floor. We walk in and there is no bop band, only a karaoke bar stocked with silver slot machines.

A man with one leg is lip-synching to a Frank Sinatra cover, "Chicago."

Grandma and I do our own combination of swing, waltz, and the intangible passion of the tango. Grandma holds me and we move to a fast one-two.

We are on the ground floor of La Coupelle restaurant in Montparnasse. This karaoke bar is our La Coupelle, where older women came to pick up young men on Sundays in the 1920's.

Grandma is light as air. She spins me around in all directions. I hold onto her hands tightly. I take the dance very seriously. We stare into each other's eyes and dissolve rhythmically from step to step. The bop music dictates our beat, and we let our feet become slow, slow, fast, fast.

Our dance is more like the tango, where everything is surrendered. I give myself to Grandma. It's the safest embrace in the world.

–Joshua Miller, The Mao Game

Loretta Callis

BY MARILU HENNER, ACTRESS

My sons have an extraordinary grandmother, though they will never meet her. Just as my grandmothers died before I knew them, my mother, Loretta Callis, died before her grandchildren were born. She would have been full of great insights and love for her grandsons. I will make sure that they get to know her through me.

When I was a young girl, my mother had an answer for my every question and advice for my every concern. However, my boys will be unable to benefit from some of the *best* advice she gave me, advice that only a girl could appreciate:

"Don't wear a bra until you're at least a B-cup, otherwise it will stunt your growth. Training bras smash you in and keep you from developing."

"You shouldn't be a cheerleader, it will hurt your female organs—all that pounding."

"Don't date a boy unless he has sisters or can dance."

"Always wear a little lipstick, it will brighten your face."

Her number one rule: "Always have a spare." (Whether it be a tire or a boy.)

❧ —— ☙

Leila Fisher

HOH ELDER AND GRANDMOTHER
in her own words

They're singing songs of the earth. . . . I'm too weak to go out there with them, but I love hearing the children's voices sing those songs. I helped teach them, you know. They're my children. All children are my children. I teach them songs and whatever else I can. That's what Grand-mothers are for–to teach songs and tell stories and show them the right berries to pick and roots to dig. And also to give them all the love they can stand. No better job in the world than being a Grandmother! . . . I'll tell you just one little story. It's one of my favorites–and it's true.

Did you ever wonder how wisdom comes? . . . There was a man, a postman here on the reservation, who heard some of the Elders talking about receiving objects that bring great power. He didn't know much about such things, but he thought to himself that it would be a wonderful thing if he could receive such an object–which can only be bestowed by the Creator. In particular, he heard from the Elders that the highest such object a person can receive is an eagle feather. He decided that was the one for him. If he could just receive an eagle feather he would have all the power and wisdom and prestige he desired. But he knew he couldn't buy one and he couldn't ask anyone to give him one. It just had to come to him somehow by the Creator's will.

Day after day he went around looking for an eagle feather. He figured one would come his way if he just kept his eyes open. It got so he thought of nothing else. That eagle feather occupied his thoughts from sunup to sundown. Weeks passed, then months, then years. Every day the postman did his rounds, always looking for that eagle feather–looking just as hard as he could. He paid no attention to his family or friends. He just kept his mind fixed on that eagle feather. But it never seemed to come. He started to grow old, but still no feather. Finally, he came to realize that no matter how hard he looked he was no closer to getting the feather than he had been the day he started.

One day he took a break by the side of the road. He got out of his little jeep mail-carrier and had a talk with the Creator. He said: "I'm so tired of looking for that eagle feather. Maybe I'm not supposed to get one. I've spent all my life thinking about that feather. I've hardly given a thought to my family and friends. All I cared about was that feather, and now life has just about passed me by. I've missed out on a lot of good things. Well, I'm giving up the search. I'm going to stop looking for that feather and start living. Maybe I have enough time left to make it up to my family and friends. Forgive me for the way I have conducted my life."

Then–and only then–a great peace came into him. He suddenly felt better inside than he had in all these years. Just as he finished his talk with the Creator and started getting back in his jeep, he was surprised by a shadow passing over him. Holding his hands over his eyes, he looked up into the sky and saw, high above, a great bird flying over. Almost instantly it disappeared. Then he saw something float down ever so lightly on the breeze–a beautiful tail feather. It was his eagle feather! He realized that the feather had come not a single moment before he had stopped searching and made peace with his Creator.

He finally learned that wisdom comes only when you stop looking for it and truly start living the life the Creator intended for you.

That postman is still alive and he's a changed person. People come to him for wisdom now and he shares everything he knows. Even though now he has the power and the prestige he searched for, he no longer cares about such things. He's concerned about others, not himself. So now you know how wisdom comes.

If anyone causes me a moment's sorrow I shall give him a lifetime's misery."

–*FORMER EMPEROR AISIN-GIORO PU LI*
QUOTING HIS GRANDMOTHER

As for promiscuity, what girl likes to feel like a piece of rock salt licked by all the passing cattle?"

–*TIM HOCKENBERRY, MUSICIAN*
ADVICE FROM HIS GRANDMOTHER

Katherine Tomlinson and Katherine Moore Mullins.

Katherine Moore Mullins

BY KATHERINE TOMLINSON,
SCREENWRITER

In addition to giving me her name (I'm a fifth generation Katherine), my grandmother passed on a piece of advice so pithy she cross-stitched it on a sampler: "Use it up. Wear it out. Make it do. Or do without."

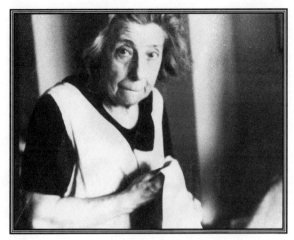

Filomena "Ox" Vigliano.

Filomena Vigliano

BY DAVID VIGLIANO,
LITERARY AGENT

When I first came home on Thanksgiving of my first year at Harvard Business School my grandmother asked me how things were going.

"Hard, Ox, very hard," I said. This was the same response I'd given others and invariably, I was met with a knowing, sympathetic nod. My grandmother, however, had no patience for people who took themselves too seriously.

"Ya got brains ... *use 'em*," she answered, in an early version of tough love before it was fashionable.

Hence a valuable lesson about taking myself too seriously.

~~ —— ~~

*E*n boca cerrado no etran moscas. (In a closed mouth, flies will not enter.)"

—SUSAN RIOS, SOCIAL WORKER
ADVICE FROM HER GRANDMOTHER LOLA RIOS

~~ —— ~~

David Craig with Leah "Bubbie" Solomon.

Leah Solomon

BY DAVID CRAIG, FILM AND
TELEVISION DEVELOPMENT EXECUTIVE

From the minute I left the womb, Bubbie offered one unconditional guarantee: I would be her favorite grand-child. To this day, as far as Bubbie is concerned, I can do no wrong. I am the smartest. I am the most clever. I can leap buildings in a single bound. This had been an honor afforded exclusively to me, her second grandson, and to no one else. It is the bedrock upon which I've built much of my life.

When I was younger, Bubbie would often ask rhetori-cally, "I bet you have to sweep the ladies away with a broom." I would just shuffle my feet, chuckle, and smile. And, in the back of my mind, I thought, "little does she know." But soon the day would come when I would have to tell her the truth: "Bubbie, I'm gay."

It was May of 1988. In the six years since Grandpa died, Bubbie had developed an independent streak, taking trips abroad, buying computers for the bookkeeping service she started when she was sixty-five; going out dancing; changing her hair color to all shades of pastel. She was quite the whipper-snapper for a woman in her eighties. So, when she called to say that she had decided to come visit me in Los Angeles for a week, I knew there was no stopping her.

In fact, I was elated. There were all sorts of things that I planned to do with her. I rented her a room at a bed and breakfast, booked her on tour buses, planned a birthday dinner, bought tickets to see Ella Fitzgerald at the Greek Theater, and scheduled a visit to Grauman's Chinese Theater. But the greatest of my plans was to come out to her. Part of what motivated this decision was that, after six years out of the closet, I had finally fallen in love.

No sooner had Bubbie arrived at the airport than I whisked her off to Canter's for her favorite meal of corned beef. She had long denounced the lack of delis in her home-town of Charlotte, North Carolina. Born and raised in Brooklyn, she missed the smell of sour pickles and whitefish.

While I hadn't planned to tell her the news right away, I figured I couldn't catch her in a better frame of mind than with sweet mustard dripping out of the corners of her mouth. So, in mid-bite, I blurted out, "Guess what, Bubbie, I'm in love." Right on cue, she leaped up and screamed, "So tell me, who *is* she? What's her name?" "Her name is Brian," I replied. (If pauses were pregnant, this one was full term.)

But I couldn't just leave it there. I had to keep babbling so the silence wouldn't make me crazy. "That's right. I'm gay. But I don't want that to change the way you feel about me, Bubbie. I'm still your favorite, right? You still love me, don't you?" Pause.

Then, with a steely resolve I've never quite seen before or since, she put down her corned beef and rye and said: "Of course I love you. Nothing you ever do will change that. I just want to know one thing. Are you happy? Because that's all that matters to me."

Then we dispensed with the formalities and she began asking question after question about Brian. "Is he Jewish? How'd you meet?" After lunch, I ran to the pay phone to tell Brian how things had gone. In my exuberance, I confessed for the first time that I loved him.

After Bubbie returned to North Carolina, she became a fearless gay and lesbian activist alongside my mother. She was treasurer of PFLAG (Parents and Friends of Lesbians and Gays). I'm told that she's their secret weapon. Whenever parents are having a particularly difficult time with their son or daughter's sexuality, Bubbie is called in on the job. "What's your problem?" she'll ask. "Do you love your child? Then get over it. They're still your child."

All it took was knowing how happy Brian made me for Bubbie to love him and instantly adopt him as her own. Over

the next five years, Bubbie became one of our greatest sup-
porters. She walked us both down the aisle at our commit-
ment ceremony. She knit afghans for our ratty old couch.

That's what made it so difficult to tell her he was dying.
But, as testament to her love for me and Brian, she was there
all the way, standing by my side at his memorial service just a
few years later. And, as I eavesdropped on her talking at the
reception, I could hear her say, "You know, that Brian was so
handsome. He was the smartest. He could do no wrong. He
could leap over buildings in a single bound."

❧ —— ☙

Dubba Markova

BY DAWNA MARKOVA, WRITER

Everyone has an island in their heart," she said, "but most
people forget when they grow up. You know eventually
each of us loses everything that's precious to us, at least on
the outside. That's just the way life is meant to be. But what
is on the island is ours to keep forever. So it's important, very
important, to really enjoy what we love, to absorb it so
deeply into you that it will take root on the island. Then it
belongs to you forever."

Shoosh. It's not polite to talk while someone else is speaking. Listen."

-TERRY BRADSHAW, SPORTS COMMENTATOR
QUOTING HIS GRANDMOTHER LOULA ESTELLE GAY

~∗ —— ∗~

Ruth Sumiko Matsuzawa Ikeda

BY STEWART IKEDA, AUTHOR OF
WHAT THE SCARECROW SAID

My grandmother is a secret polyglot: English is her native tongue–she speaks it well, types and writes it better. Japanese is the antique card game she played as a girl– the hand-painted, gilt-edged cards of poetry in *hiragana*, tucked in a silk-wrapped box, precious but dusty, for there's no one else to play it with her. The Little-Said is her language of instruction–it rings louder than a pat on the back, a slap, or a kiss. In the Unsaid echoes secret wisdom.

"When I was your age," she begins–the usual Depression-era Grandma fare–"I rose at dawn to work at the nursery before school. After classes, I worked as a mother's helper." She dispenses these chestnuts only rarely, knowing that a tree-load of such wisdoms at best produces inward groans in

Stewart David Ikeda with his grandmother
Ruth Sumiko Matsuzawa Ikeda.

spoiled grandchildren. Grandma is economical, resourceful, and clever in everything—with words, too.

In 1970-something, she enters the den from the kitchen and tells me to get dressed for grocery shopping. A Saturday: I've spent every other weekend with my grandparents after my folks divorced. I am stuck in the position I've held—lying on my stomach, the fleshy cheeks propped up on my fists gouged with knuckle indentations—through five hours of cartoons. "Doan-wannagododastore," I slur, and she easily deciphers my garble.

"What if *I* said I didn't want to go," she posits, "next time *you* wanted to go somewhere?" And her *What if* resounds like the thunder itself, simply because she has never denied me ... anything. I have never, ever heard her say "no." She taught me how too many words can weaken, a few can pack a punch, and things left unsaid can have enormous power.

"No" was the Never-said and "No" was the silenced. "No" was the Japanese she learned to not-speak. "No" was Sumiko, the given name she chose to replace with Ruth. "No" was the refusal to dignify her neighbors' hysterical charges with a response; it was the protest she did not mount against her incarceration as "the Enemy." "When I was your age," she will admonish her grandchildren, "I had to walk a mile to school every day and a mile back." But what an overwhelming "No" underlies the tale she never told us: *When I was young, about your age, I walked the length and breadth of the Arizona desert internment camp, waiting for my life beyond the barbed wire to begin.*

"No" was also the disappointment that she kept to herself for fifty years, the cynicism she refused to bequeath to her family.

What she can't tell me, she shows me. In 1990-something, on a dark-skied winter day at the Joshua Tree National Park, the safe white barge of her Buick is dwarfed by the desert between Arizona and California. It's not our destination; by the odometer, we've a good half-century yet to go on this road trip, driving in reverse all the way. Rather, it's just a pit-stop, a photo-op as we begin to recover her story. The viewfinder shows a small-boned, graceful woman, tightly wrapped in a windbreaker so tidy, it's as if it came right out of the cleaners; and wrapped in a hug by her own slender arms; and wrapped by nervousness in this first adventure of her widowhood.

I want words to commemorate her dignity, our moment together, and this act of love. I want to say I think no one in America belongs less to these hills, where the dust does not stick to her at all. I want to know how she feels. I want to thank her for paving the way to my life, then for taking me back through hers. She always says she can't tell me much–that she doesn't really remember that part of her life any-more. But I think I do.

So instead I take the picture. Some things, we know, are stronger left unsaid.

❧ —— ❧

Isabelle Wykoff Totto

BY GEORGIA O'KEEFFE, PAINTER (1887–1986)

Grandmother Totto, a tall dignified woman, beautiful in bearing, with masses of white hair and most particular ways, kept in her parlor "whatnots" with fine ornaments. I would play with them and when she would say firmly, "You must not do that a-gain," I was so fascinated by her precise way of speaking that I would do it again just to hear her say it.

Mary Nina Kack

BY VALERIE KACK-BRICE, EDITOR,
WRITER, AND SOCIAL WORKER

S he was the first one to teach me about guilt. That, of course, was only a small gift from this grandmother. There were other things like permission to follow one's heart, like she did to marry my grandfather, out of the tuberculosis ward, out of the convent. It wasn't a big guilt she taught me, just enough for a four-year-old to sting a little. Mary Nina probably weighed over three hundred pounds and on her small frame, she looked more round than a peach. I was fascinated by her form. It dominated my experience of her. More so than the porcelain Madonnas she painted in sky blue and white lace. More so than the black 1932 Model T she drove to get eggs.

What I wondered one day when she cared for me while my sister was being born, was what she wore *under* her big round black skirts. Surely they didn't make pink polka dotted panties like I wore in her size. And surely, the white bras my mother wore couldn't be nearly enough to harness those huge face-crushing breasts. Did she wear diapers like my little sister would wear? Being a clever four year old, I figured I was entitled to know.

I schemed to catch her unaware and called her to look out the window at some unimportant detail I had identified to distract her. I dropped my rubber doll and kicked it under the sideboard and naturally had to get down on the floor to retrieve it. This required reaching way under. I had to turn my head (so I could see up her skirt). I was scared and ashamed, and only glanced upward then grabbed the arm of my doll and quickly pulled her out. Once standing, to my dismay, I realized I didn't know what I had seen. There were folds of cloth under there, but no true, clearly defined form of anything that looked like panties.

Though what I later learned to be guilt was nudging at my consciousness, I waited a day and plotted another research expedition. This time, I attacked from below while she prepared the biscuit dough at the kitchen table. Sitting under the table, I could feel the shame rising to my face but was compelled to finish what I started. Although she was still a stranger to me, I knew she loved me. That deserved some kind of loyalty.

Halfheartedly, the ball rolled out of my hands and rested against the edge of her shoe. Perfect. I stared at it a long time. My mind fought to connect that foot to the folds of . . . something which connected to my grandmother, the peach. I don't believe that anyone ever taught me that it was impolite to look under a woman's skirt, but somehow, I knew that what I was doing was wrong. My ball rocked against her foot as she stirred and kneaded. I felt sad. Only later was I to understand that my wickedness was probably more about missing my mother and fear about who would be coming home with her to take my place. Then, I only knew hurt from having to harness my curiosity with the sting of betrayal. In my mind, what I was doing had gotten complicated too by my remembering that she had been a nun. What I felt was surely the pinprick of God's wrath. I couldn't do it. I reached for the ball without looking up and said, "Grandma, can I help you make biscuits?" I could. We did. And until she died, I remained only slightly curious and then, a little jealous of the undertaker. He was a real stranger and knew more about her than I ever would.

❧ —— ☙

Ruth Busby

BY TINA TOUCHSTONE, WRITER

Ever since my grandfather died two years ago, my grandmother has been worrying the family with her newly found assertiveness. The same woman who never said no to anyone is now saying it as much as she pleases, which is often. But her assertiveness has paid off.

Grandma has always had a hard time remembering where she has written my telephone number. A few weeks ago when I called her she asked me again for my number. Then Grandma told me to hang on the line. After holding a few minutes, I heard some pounding. It seems Grandma had gotten a hammer and nailed my number to her wall. Now she calls me anytime she wants.

Your mother may not be as stupid as you think, but you may not find this out until you're a mother yourself. However, I do hope you learn this lesson a great deal sooner. Believe it or not, mothers often know best."

–EILEEN FORD, CO-FOUNDER OF FORD MODELS
ADVICE FROM HER GREAT-GRANDMOTHER LAINE

Anabelle England

BY VICKI PHILLIPS, WRITER

Anabelle England, my maternal grandmother, had only an eighth-grade education, but this never stopped her from imparting to me the wisdom born of life experience. Grandma, a widow, lived on a farm.

She read widely and freely and encouraged me to do the same. In fact, we read a book together every week as a matter of principle. Her advice to me on my thirteenth birthday–both the last year I knew her, and the first year I had a boyfriend: "Dating is fine, but when night falls, take a book to bed. You'll learn more that way."

If your baby is "beautiful and perfect, never cries or fusses, sleeps on schedule and burps on demand, an angel all the time" . . . you're the grandma.

–*Teresa Bloomingdale, writer*

Mamie Eisenhower

BY SUSAN EISENHOWER,
WRITER AND POLITICAL ANALYST

My grandmother] accommodated the third floor of the White House for our frequent visits: she had made over one of the larger rooms as a playroom, and the solarium at the very top of the Executive Mansion was a sitting and dining room for us when we visited. Mamie kept three birds there for our enjoyment, a canary and two parakeets: Gabby, High Glory, and Pete. When Pete died, she allowed us to give him a solemn burial on the edge of what is now the Rose Garden.

She kept bicycles and an electric miniature of a Thunderbird car for us to ride up and down the ground-floor hallways when the morning tours were over. She also welcomed us into her room after her staff meetings, and we would rummage through the knickknacks she kept for us on her side table. She could be a captivating grandmother; her shimmering blue eyes held you in their enchanting grip while she imparted secrets and planned conspiracies.

But even as very young children, we knew that the rules in Mamie's house were to be strictly obeyed. No running up and down corridors, no sliding down banisters, no greasy fingers on the woodwork, no getting down from the table before the meal was over. All of us were strictly schooled in manners, and Mamie even taught us to use finger bowls properly by the time we were three years old. We would receive admonitions about drying our hair after swimming in the White House pool, and lectures about wearing warm clothing when we went out to play—scolding about wet heads and inadequate clothing coming, perhaps, from her reflexive fear about our health and well-being. And, though unknown to us at the time, whenever the Secret Service drove us somewhere, she would always make a point of telling them to drive very carefully, "Let's have no more tragedies," she would say.

As the years progressed, she increasingly relied on reminiscences for sustenance, remarking in a letter [to me]:

You children were all more like Ike's and my children than our grandchildren and have meant so much to us all through the years. I was thankful when Ike finally died that he had the opportunity of knowing each one of you but sorry he did not know his great-grandchildren . . . I often look at your wedding pictures and live over the night that you were married, the supper party here, and the things that went on which were really quite humorous in afterthought. This house has known many happy times, like your wedding supper, along with other sorrows. In other words—it is home.

She was a friend to many, but also to us. Her philosophy, honed over years of hardship, was something we kept with us, that stays with us still. When someone passed on gossip about one of her friends, she'd dismiss it by saying, "Oh I don't believe that." If told that a friend of hers was using her, she'd reply gaily, "And I'm using her! She makes me laugh." If things bothered us or brought us low, she'd exclaim, "Just throw it over your shoulder." But most of all, she defended those she loved, and she loved fiercely.

Rose Rodriquez

BY TRICIA IALEGGIO, WRITER

Italian wakes are well known for the loud weeping and wailing of its women mourners. "Oh, why didn't the Lord take me instead?" At one such family funeral, my dad approached Great-Grandma Rose. "Grandma, if the Lord *did* come to take you instead, what would you do?"

Without missing a beat, great-grandma replied, "I'd tell him to go next door."

You remember thinking while braiding your hair that you look a lot like your mother. Your mother, who looked like your grandmother and her grandmother before her. Your mother, she introduced you to the first echoes of the tongue that you now speak when at the end of the day she would braid your hair while you sat between her legs, scrubbing the kitchen pots. While your fingers worked away at the last shadows of her day's work, she would make your braids Sunday-pretty, even during the week.

When she was done she would ask you to name each braid after those nine hundred and ninety-nine women who were boiling in your blood, and since you had written them down and memorized them, the names would come rolling off your tongue. And this was your testament to the way that these women lived and died and lived again.

—*EDWIDGE DANTICAT,* KRIK? KRAK!

❧ —— ❧

Mary Ethel Bates and Cecile Norwood

BY BRANDY, SINGER AND ACTRESS

From the time I was a baby, Mary Ethel Bates, my maternal grandmother, loved to hold me in her arms and sing to me. I am told that every day she scooped me up, laid me in her lap, and sang to me, often for hours on end. Grandma claims that even before I was walking or talking I sang back to her, "cooing and caaing in tune." Although this may be a *grandmother's* memory speaking, there is no doubt that she has always been a powerful presence in my life. Grandma is a very strong and religious person, always teaching me to seek God first, love my enemies, and to keep striving for my goals. Her love is steady, constant.

Though my father's mother lived farther away, she never failed to show her love or support. I remember our family

Brandy and her grandmother Mary Ethel Bates.

piling into the car to take the long scenic drives to Grandma's home in Greenwood. My Grandmother Norwood loves to hear me sing and has always encouraged me. She told me stories about my father's side of the family and of his childhood. I am grateful to her for raising her son to be the wonderful father and man he is today. I am truly blessed to know both of my grandmothers. In their own ways, they have and always will be special parts of my life.

Christine Hamp Zacharias

BY AGNES ASH,
PUBLISHER AND JOURNALIST

Grandma lived with us when I was a small child growing up and starting school in Manhattan. In the early days of the Depression, we lived on 178th Street, an upper-middle-class block where some apartment buildings carried the elite label "elevator buildings." One day we woke to find huge steel girders, painted orange and stretching from one end of the block to the other, piled six feet high along the curb. The George Washington Bridge was beginning construction. I went out to balance walk along this exciting jungle gym.

A boy from the next building, about my age but much larger and much better coordinated, climbed up the wooden milk boxes appropriated as makeshift stairs, and followed me on the beam. I made a friendly remark in German and then told him I would get off as soon as I reached the other end. Obviously, I wasn't good at this sport. He pushed me off, shouting "This is an English neighborhood."

I skinned my knees and went crying to Grandma who painted on iodine and lectured me. "He was hostile to you because you didn't speak his language. He didn't know what you were saying. You speak English. You were not smart.

Don't let bullies push you around but don't ever respond to anyone who is different from you with a fist. That sort of reaction will bring you more grief and you will miss out on so much that there is to learn in this world."

Then her tone mellowed and she continued, "You learned a song in Sunday school that teaches the same lesson. Now sing it for me, I'll hum along."

I knew instantly which song she meant and sang it in my off-key voice while she hummed in monotone. Neither of us was musical.

Jesus died for all the children, all the children of the world.
Black or yellow, red or white, they are precious in his sight
Jesus died for all the children in the world.

"Now can you understand that, Agnes? Even if they don't know about our religion, other people probably know about one that teaches the same thing."

Decades later in Atlanta, Georgia, I stood looking over the shoulder of Ralph McGill, a Pulitzer Prize–winning editor who fought segregation, while he read the news coming over the Associated Press wire, the text of the Supreme Court decision on school integration. He didn't look jubilant, just worried about the reaction to follow. Not being American-born, I felt genetically unqualified to intrude on this historic moment. School integration seemed a small step to me. As I walked silently down the hall back to my own desk, my throat tightened and that children's hymn repeated over and over in my head. It wasn't an intellectual response, but it was emotional and illustrative of the power of basic morality learned in childhood.

❧ —— ❦

Carrie Jamison Whittaker

BY CAROLYN S. MATEER, WRITER

One special moment with [my grandmother] Carrie Jamison Whittaker is indelibly etched in my memory. We were alone in her cavernous kitchen after a family dinner. It must have been a gathering of some consequence, a special birthday or anniversary. The table had been set with her only posses-sions of any real value: a set of china passed down from some more affluent ancestor. Whether the dishes were Spode or Wedgwood, or simply the product of some local Pennsylvania potter, I knew they were valued beyond anything else in that simple house, and were perhaps the only things she owned of any material significance. Of far greater importance was the fact that she loved them. I had seen her hold a dish to the light to catch the play of sunshine on the blues and golds of the dainty floral pattern so typical of nineteenth-century dinnerware.

I was no more than six, hanging on her skirts, anxious for the table clearing and dish-washing to be over so I could cuddle in her ample lap for a story and a hug. Eager to move things along, I carried plates from the table to the sink to be scraped, despite the apprehensive glances shot my way. The worst happened. The vegetable dish slipped from my hands, scattering broken glass and bits of corn across the worn linoleum. I had an instant feeling of sharp inner pain, worse than I had ever experienced from a cut finger or a scraped knee. For the first time in my life, I came face to face with true anguish, guilt that could never be totally resolved.

For one long moment there was silence, broken only when sobs came pouring out from deep in my throat. She looked at me for an additional second or two, and then, picking me up and heading for the rocker in the window, said, "I'm glad you broke that dish; I was getting tired of it."

We turn not older with the years but newer every day.
—EMILY DICKINSON, POET

(Left to right) *Muriel Palitz, Suzy Palitz, and Edith Dobson in 1964.*

D on't sleep with your socks on. You'll wake up with webbed feet!"

−SUZY PALITZ, PSYCHOLOGIST
ADVICE FROM HER GRANDMOTHER EDITH DOBSON

Ariadni Stassinopoulos

BY ARIANNA HUFFINGTON, COLUMNIST

I never met my maternal grandmother, who came to Greece as a refugee from Russia during the Revolution in 1918. But she has been a real presence in my life, because my mother has always been so full of stories, sayings, and aphorisms. My favorite saying of hers—which my mother repeated endlessly to my sister and me—was: "Angels fly because they take themselves lightly."

I keep returning to my grandmother's wisdom whenever I lose perspective and let life grow heavy, between the expectations I place on myself and those imposed by others. So when the juggling act between children and work, travel and home, action and quiet time gets too hard, I think of those angels who fly above it all because they take themselves lightly.

NURTURING

Mama Cile with her grandson Alan.

Lucille Jackson

BY ALAN JACKSON,
SINGER AND MUSICIAN

I grew up next door to Mama Cile, and what I remember most is that she always made me fried apple pies. We were real close, so close, that she even broke her arm to make me feel better about breaking mine. Naw, just kidding, it was really just a coincidence, but this is my favorite picture of my grandmother and me.

Always eat dinner before you go out because it is very unfeminine to eat like a horse."

–VERA WANG, DESIGNER
ADVICE FROM HER GRANDMOTHER

❧ —— ❧

If God had intended us to follow recipes, He wouldn't have given us grandmothers.

–LINDA HENLEY, WRITER

❧ —— ❧

Eva Crowell

BY BRADLEY OGDEN, CHEF

Some of my earliest and most memorable taste experiences took place during the summers that my brothers and I were treated to the delights of Grandma Eva's farm. Antici-pation of these visits kept us excited for months.

Awaiting us were glorious picnics deep in Grandma's fields. Beneath towering cornstalks, we feasted on her home-made fried chicken and plump, vine-ripened tomatoes, still

Eva Crowell.

warm from the sun. Dessert at Grandma Eva's always held the promise of her wonderful fruit pies–fresh rhubarb, apple, cherry, strawberry, as well as every variety of wild berry. All day I dreamt of the gorgeous pies cooling on Grandma's kitchen window sill. After dinner, I knew one would be waiting for me. I loved to pick rhubarb from her garden. Sometimes, before Grandma could even get the rhubarb into her pies, I dipped the fresh stalks in sugar and ate them raw.

These unforgettable chapters of my childhood were instrumental in developing my food preferences and lifestyle. Later in life I realized that the simple pleasures cherished during idyllic summers at Grandma Eva's were the seeds of my culinary motivation and inspiration. I have never lost my appreciation for basic, pure tastes, from fresh stream trout and free-range chicken to hand-picked fruits and vegetables. To this day, my philosophy remains: Keep it simple, use the freshest ingredients available, and put them together in such a way that the flavors, colors, and textures combine to bring out the best in each other—a philosophy born in the fields and in the kitchen of my grandmother many years ago.

❧ —— ❧

No matter what your age is ... chocolate milk cures everything."

−OLIVER STONE, DIRECTOR
ADVICE FROM HIS GRANDMOTHER ADELE PAULINE GODDET

❧ —— ❧

Lucy's father, Jim Lehrer; her mother, Kate; her aunt Joan; and Gaga
(left to right) *at Lucy's high school graduation.*

Lucy Staples

BY LUCY TOM LEHRER, PLAYWRIGHT

Those Cowboys ain't worth a damn today. You know, that Tom Landry is a religious man. So is that Roger Staubach." These were things my grandmother, Gaga, used to say on Sunday afternoons when my sisters and I would sit around the TV set with her in her Dallas apartment. Her words were as comforting and familiar as the lingering smell of fried chicken from that day's lunch.

Sometimes I'd get frightened when she'd stand up and holler at the TV set during a Cowboys' game. Often she'd stomp across the room and turn that TV set off with such venom you'd think they'd just announced that a Republican had been elected President.

I loved the sound of the game in the background while I closed my eyes for a lazy daydreaming/nap lying next to her on the couch. Even now, I love to doze with the sounds of a football game on in the background. It transports me to the childhood feeling that there is order in the world, at least for a few hours. Everyone can care about one thing for a little while . . . who will win the game.

At a playoffs party with fellow native Texans last season, I found myself caring a great deal about who would win the game. It was as if Gaga's spirit had risen up in me. At times I was jumping off of my chair and yelling at the players in the TV set to "Run!" and "Get him!" The muscles in my neck and shoulders became tense every time the other team was about to score.

And while I'm on the subject of TV sets, Gaga used to say that we don't say we *hate* anything, not even our TV set. Although Gaga hasn't talked for a few years, she was at one time a strong, bossy Texas woman who supported my mother by working for Sears and Roebuck for twenty-seven years. She'd spend the week driving around Texas for work and then return to Dallas on Fridays. She came by our house to pick me and my sisters up and take us to the Pig Stand for pig sandwiches, french fries and chocolate milk shakes. After we ordered, she would say to the waitress, "Their eyes are bigger than their stomachs."

Gaga had a way of talking to waitresses and sales clerks that made my sisters and me cringe with embarrassment. She would announce to perfect strangers that she and I were the "two Lucy's" since I was her namesake. She'd also let them know that I wanted everything that was pink and that if "her Gaga is around she knows she'll get it." I was forever fighting the urge to say to her, "Gaga, they just don't care," but I never did.

Gaga took her politics seriously. She didn't think any president was worth a damn since Roosevelt. She was proud of the fact that she'd worked for the WPA and she announced this at any opportunity. When Aunt Katie, one of her six sisters, became a Republican, I remember Gaga spent an entire evening sitting in her car with her purse clutched tightly against her chest until the rest of us had finished dinner. Apparently, a political discussion had started and Gaga "just got burned up."

Now when I visit Gaga, I talk to her about things we used to do, and I don't know if she hears me. Sometimes I see a little tear start to form in her eyes and I think I might be getting through. The strength of her fierce independence and stubbornness will never be gone . . . not as long as I'm around.

Eleanor Schneider

CHEF, GRANDMOTHER,
AND GREAT-GRANDMOTHER
in her own words

Though I grew up in a very wealthy family in New York City, I married a poor man. We eloped. My husband graduated from MIT with honors but no one wanted to hire a Jewish engineer in those days. He was a fine and honorable man. I had a very poor married life financially, but a very happy one. My husband died at the age of forty-six. I had to work because I had three children to raise and put through school. I am in my ninety-second year and I am still doing what I have to do! I am a workaholic. I cannot be idle. I don't understand all these old people sitting around watching television. My doctor tells me, "God knows what you're doing, but whatever you're doing–don't stop. You'll live another fifty years!" "God forbid!" I told him. But I am a happy person. Life is great. We don't know what is in store for us. We have to accept what it has to offer.

Two years ago my son took our family to Le Pescadou, a lovely French restaurant in Greenwich Village for a birthday dinner. One of my grandchildren happened to be holding a box of my homemade truffles. The chef caught a glimpse of them and asked, "What have you got there?" My grandchild offered her a truffle and she sampled one. "Where did you get these?" she asked. "My grandma makes them," came the reply. "Well, tell your grandmother to come see me!" And I've been filling orders for that restaurant ever since. People tell me that a very famous actress secretly buys my truffles—but no one will say who she is because she has a very health-conscious image! The actress said, "Go back and tell whoever made these truffles that they are simply wonderful. I've never tasted anything like them! But she's a terrible business-woman. I usually pay forty dollars a pound—and these are much better!" I took it with a grain of salt.

I began making truffles a few years ago when I went into one of the New York City gourmet grocers and saw their truffle recipe. Forty dollars a pound—but how good can they be? I thought. They use condensed milk and did not use the proper chocolate! I figured, "I'll try to improve on this." And I did. But the recipe is *my* secret. Years ago, I was injured and lost my sense of taste and smell. So when I finish a batch of truffles, I call my son Bobby who lives upstairs to come down and taste them. I don't sell them until I know they're perfect. I don't cheat. I only use ingredients that are pure—only the best.

I have six wonderful grandchildren and two great-grandchildren. When my grandchildren started to make their own money, I took them aside: "Listen kids, you have an example in your old grandmother. No matter how much money you make, put some aside. Don't spend like a drunken sailor! Think twice before you spend money on something that is not necessary. You do not know what the future holds for you. You must be prepared. You see this in me."

But, in the end, I have what money can't buy: good family relationships. There is nothing more precious in the world.

❦ —— ❧

Grace Rice Steed

BY ALLISON ANDERS, FILM DIRECTOR

We called her *mamaw,* a Southern term for grandmother that probably came from a Cherokee or Creek word. Not many people use this endearment; I have only ever heard two other people use it–Jimmy Swaggart and Ashley Judd. Ironically, Ashley's mamaw lived in the same little Ohio river town of Ashland, Kentucky, where my mamaw and I lived, the town where I was born.

My mamaw was my favorite person to be with, without a doubt. She was already in her sixties when I was born in 1954. My Mamaw Steed was in her forties when my mother, the last of her eight daughters, was born. Mamaw was the daughter of a Baptist preacher and his weary, quiet wife. She had ten sisters and four brothers, and they lived on a farm in Elliot County, Kentucky. Little is known of what her childhood was like. It is as if my mamaw's life began at fourteen, when she was raped. This event completely dominated the rest of her life.

She was delivering milk to the local residents during the winter when a man invited her in from the snow to warm herself. He fed her a cup of warm milk, and this was the last thing she remembered. She had been drugged and raped and discarded in the snow. I always wonder about the details—I wonder how she felt the next day or later that night, if she had bruises or wounds—probably not, if she was drugged. But I am sure she knew something painful had happened to her—even if it just stung when she peed. If she hadn't been awake during the rape—did she still feel dirty, did she want to wash herself over and over again? But these are all things I'll never know.

I imagine she went on with her life, in some vague discomfort for the next few months, maybe declining to deliver milk to Mr. Pennington, or maybe just "accidentally on purpose" forgetting his address. But within months it became obvious that my mamaw, Grace Rice, was pregnant. Upon learning of her condition, her father beat her severely; some say he even kicked her in the stomach. She was banished to a small room in the farmhouse for the remainder of her pregnancy. She was allowed no visitors; she was not permitted to eat meals with the rest of the family. She was their great shame.

She was given no information on how babies were conceived or born. She was told she was going to be a mother, but she had no idea what would happen to her during child-birth. She told her own daughters later, recalling her state of mind at age fourteen, that she had seen animals on the farm give birth and she had just assumed that was how she would do it—crawl up in a corner and have a litter. Well, she did give birth in something of a corner, in that miserable little room, with a midwife attending, and although she did not have a litter, she did have twin daughters, whom she named Mae and Fae.

After her daughters were born, my mamaw was allowed to work on the farm. But the twins were never allowed out of the room when her father was present—he never wanted to lay eyes on those bastard children. Family legend has it that one day, when the babies were just past their first birthday, a neighbor came to visit and asked about the twins. To my mamaw's uneasy surprise, her father sternly told her to "Go fetch them babies and bring 'em down here for Mrs. so-and-so to see." When he saw the two precious little girls his eyes welled up and he fell madly in love with them and amended all the pain he had caused my mamaw by embracing them as his own. Her parents agreed to raise the children as theirs and allow my grandmother to go to the "city" to work.

She was eighteen when she met my papaw Harry Steed. He was working in a storefront in downtown Ashland when he first saw her walk past the store with her sister Alice. He winked at her, and she promptly snubbed him, literally turning up her nose. But eleven days later they were married, and they stayed married until her death at age seventy-two.

Many people say that trauma victims develop a heightened sense of intuition, even ESP. My mamaw had all of that. She predicted deaths–including the death of her own mother and two of her children: Harry Junior, her only son, who was hit by a streetcar at age six; and Joanne, her eighteen-year-old daughter, who had just given birth to her first baby. When my mamaw's mother died, my mamaw apparently had a vision. She was distraught over what to do with her twins, who were now twelve. Her husband refused to accept the girls and would not allow her to bring them to live with him. But now with their mother dead, her sister Molly had offered to adopt the girls herself, something that broke my mamaw's heart. Days after her mother's death, she was sitting at the kitchen table in tears, worried over what to do with her twin daughters. Her mother appeared to her and told her to defy her sister and her husband and bring those children to live with her. And she did just that, risking her marriage for these twins, who were conceived during a rape. Nonetheless, these were her daughters and she loved them.

My mamaw could predict everything of major importance in the lives of the people around her–and of little importance, too. She could also read auras, without knowing this is what she was doing–she would simply refuse to be in the same room with certain people due to the color of the aura around them. When I was a child, there was a game we played to test her psychic abilities–how many cars will it be before my mom turns that corner and comes home? How many fingers am I holding up? When exactly am I going to marry Paul McCartney? (He was her favorite, too–the woman had taste!)

When I was five, my mamaw and I watched *The Afternoon Matinee* every day on TV. The single most important movie for me was *A Stolen Life*, a melodrama starring Bette Davis as twin sisters. This film probably informed all my notions of romantic love–for better or for worse–and the importance of soulmates, destiny, and being seen for one's true self. We both loved this film, and I sat on her lap watching it, in her big chair, just her and me. When I made my film *Gas, Food, Lodging* I had unconsciously shot an ending (now no longer in the film) that was a direct rip-off of the final scene in *A Stolen Life*. Those afternoons with her were extremely precious to me and had a tremendous impact on my life and work.

She never said a single cross word to me, never raised her voice, never made me feel bad or ashamed in any way–she was incredibly tender and pure. She was a Cancer: domestic, mothering, and warm–although, surprisingly (or not so surprisingly), she was not so sensitive when her own daughters became pregnant out of wedlock, which most of them did before marrying. She was apparently the one who turned the cold shoulder and didn't want to hear about it. But once the grandchildren came, she was all over us (I was one of those conceived-out-of-wedlock babies). We were all crazy about her, everyone remembers her with warmth and fondness, and we miss her terribly.

When she died of breast cancer, I was only twelve. She had been bedridden for years with arthritis and other problems. She was said to have called my name when she died. Out of all her children and grandchildren and siblings, she only called three names: mine, my aunt Jeri's, and my cousin Mark's. I have always felt intensely blessed and burdened by this—if only I had known what it meant. Sometimes it was pulled out as a caution, or as a reprimand that I should "be a good girl 'cause your mamaw called your name when she died." Two months after her death, I also was raped, and maybe this had something to do with it. Maybe she wanted to give me strength, maybe she simply wanted to see me again. I have no idea.

It's sad to me that my children, or even my youngest sister, never got to meet her. But she watches over them nevertheless. I have no doubt that she is around me, warning me against people with bad auras—advice I need a lot in my line of work! And without a doubt, the first time I saw *A Stolen Life* in a movie theater a few years ago, there was a very warm seat next to mine.

D on't eat too much cantaloupe because you have trouble digesting it."

–ADAM SANDLER, COMEDIAN AND ACTOR
ADVICE FROM HIS GRANDMOTHER

Guadalupe Díaz

BY MARISA TREVIÑO, WRITER

My abuela, Guadalupe Díaz, had a sense of humor that permeated every aspect of her life–even the food. One day, while mashing beans to make refried beans, she stopped, thought a minute and told me (in Spanish): "You know, beans are like your worst enemies. They're always talking behind your back."

Unfortunately, over everything else this amazing woman taught me, this is the one thing I remember with clarity and a chuckle.

✦ —— ✦

Harriet Shoman

BY MARY SHOMAN,
SCREENWRITER AND WRITER

My eccentric Armenian grandmother Harriet taught me that you never get old if you don't think you are, and Harriet never thought she was old. When I was eight and she was already over sixty, Harriet, clad in leopard print pants and cat's-eye glasses, said, "Never call me Grandma again, it makes me feel too old." What was I to call her? "Call me Nanette instead." Nanette? Even Harriet wasn't her real name. She started life as Goharic, a name which I believe means "jewel" in Armenian. When she came to the United States, and started first grade in Philadelphia, no one could say "Goharic," so they started calling her Goharriet. She told them to drop the "Go," and was Harriet ever since.

Harriet had very definite opinions on male attractiveness. After her yearly solo excursions to visit her sister in San Juan, Puerto Rico, she would return with stories of friendly beach boys named José, and handsome Rauls at the slot machines. For Harriet, swarthiness was ultimate. Arabs, Latins, Indians, it didn't matter . . . they were handsome as long as they passed the Harriet skin-tone test. When I was just a child, she would point to Robert Redford on television and announce to me, "Never bring a man home like that. He's too washed out!" He has no "substance" (read "skin tone"). She'd have loved Antonio Banderas. Definitely passes the Harriet skin-tone test!

Ann Green

BY NANCY GLASS, JOURNALIST

When I would stay at my grandparents' farm, my grandmother would always let me choose what I wanted for dinner. I loved those tiny little hot dogs they sell as "cocktail franks." My grandmother was always suspicious of hot dogs. She was certain they contained something horrible. So, she would boil them, then she would bake them, then she would broil them. I would end up with a plate full of little black pellets. They tasted like charcoal bricks with a spongy center ... But I loved them. I also loved her for saying yes and making those hot dogs even though she didn't want to.

❦ —— ❦

The jelly stuff on Spam is part of the meat, so eat it."

–BILL ENGVALL, COMEDIAN AND ACTOR
ADVICE FROM HIS GRANDMOTHER MARY ENGVALL

❦ —— ❦

Eugenia Manes Cribari

BY STEPHEN J. CRIBARI, WRITER

My grandmother, Eugenia Manes Cribari, was of Albanian ancestry. She came from Falconara Albanese, in that part of Southern Italy that was Greek before it was Roman. (It has yet to become Italian, according to some of the people in the North.) Nonna arrived in America in the early 1900s with a fierce sense of family loyalty born of poverty, where survival is tenuous and safety is found first and last within family. So, in her new home, Nonna made a big family: seven boys and three girls.

Sunday was *always* dinner at Nonna's. At a table as big as the world we were surrounded by parents, siblings, aunts, uncles, cousins. And, of course, Nonna. Whatever or whoever else there was, there was always Nonna and pasta with tomato sauce and a big bowl of Parmigiano into which I'd dip a hungry finger. Usually, I'd lick it first to make sure that the cheese would stick to it. My father always objected, and Nonna always rebuked him for it. It was my first, and only, experience of absolute power. The goddess of the family at the tip of my sticky little finger.

As best I can tell, Nonna loved three things above all else: her grandchildren, her purple hydrangeas, and three old cast iron skillets. I suspect she loved these things even more than her own children. Maybe even more than God. Or maybe this was her way of loving God, of proving her fruitfulness to her Creator: the enduring fruit of her womb, the fruit of the soil, the fruit of her kitchen. Each, to her, must have been beautiful and fragrant beyond expectation.

In the last years of her life, Nonna spent most of her time staring, silently, into middle distances. Sometimes, she would reach out and stroke my head with her bony fingers. Then her eyes would focus into a fierce look. It frightened me. She was too weak to speak and I was too young to understand that she was teaching me the meaning of her name: *manes*, from the Latin verb meaning to endure, to last. I can see the look in her eyes today as clearly as I did thirty-five years ago: *stare death in the face and let it know that you still exist.*

Nonna's house has long been sold, and with it the purple hydrangeas. Without its center, the family spread out then dispersed. But I have Nonna's cast iron skillets. And her pasta pot. And her wooden bowl and her old iron *mezzaluna*. With them, the dinners I make are beautiful and fragrant beyond expectation. The fruitfulness of Nonna's womb, and the soil of her homeland, and her kitchen, enduring still.

Mary May Bell

BY LYN PAULSIN, PRESIDENT,
GEORGETTE MOSBACHER ENTERPRISES

In America in the early 1900s, independence and self-sufficiency were not virtues readily encouraged in women, particularly in the small Indiana steel town where my grandmother lived. But Mary Bell's character was shaped more by her family's needs than by cultural norms. My grandmother had to be self-reliant. With a gambling husband whom she soon divorced and no financial resources to fall back on, she had to find ways to feed and clothe her children. Her vitality and resourcefulness persisted long after her children became parents themselves. So by the time my sister and I came along, our grandmother was adept at finding creative ways to make ends meet.

Every other year throughout my childhood, Mary Bell bought a house. Inevitably, when we first laid eyes on Grandma's latest purchase, we saw a house in a serious state of disrepair. But Grandma saw potential. Our whole family pitched in to clean and paint. Soon, we were assigned jobs based on our ages and strengths. Once the house was in shape, Grandma turned it around for rent or resale.

I remember one house in particular. It had a lovely front porch with countless windows. Like all of the houses

Grandma bought, this one needed a good paint job. Each windowpane needed to be painstakingly taped before it was painted. As the youngest member of Grandma's work crew, my job was to remove the tape once the paint dried. I remember the satisfaction I felt as I pulled off each piece of tape, revealing a perfect line of fresh paint below. Another assignment I was given was to wash the paintbrushes. These were my jobs and my jobs alone. I felt a great sense of responsibility making sure that each brush was properly cleaned and dried, every last bit of tape discarded. Each of us felt a tremendous sense of importance in our individual contribution. And it wasn't all sweat and toil. While we worked, we talked and laughed. Our chores were often interrupted by water fights, dog chasing, or lunch breaks of bologna sandwiches on paper plates. Work that by other eyes might be perceived as sheer drudgery, in Grandma's world was magically transformed into pure fun.

When I look back on those days, I don't remember hard work. I remember laughter and sharing, a sense of community and accomplishment. Today, work is too often perceived as something to be dreaded or avoided. Worse yet, our labors go unappreciated or unseen. Jobs are not equally valued. Too often, pride in a good day's work is lost. Mary Bell taught me that each of us has an important contribution to make. When we work together with mutual respect, love, and laughter, even the most unloved house can become a home. With Grandma in charge, it always did.

❧ —— ❦

*John Hockenberry's great-grandmother
Nancy Barron Slagle.*

Doris Stryker Slagle, Nancy Barron Slagle, and Beatrice Eiche Hockenberry

BY JOHN HOCKENBERRY, JOURNALIST

To a kid, grandmothers reveal something that your parents would probably just as soon you not know: that mommy and daddy were also kids once. Grandmothers prove beyond doubt that those slightly grumpy people with the car keys and the house payments, who try to exercise total control over your life, were also sent to their rooms, told to eat their broccoli, and spanked for sneaking into the cookie jar. My great-grandmother showed me something more amazing, almost unbelievable for five years old, that even my grandparents had been little kids. Grandmothers are a child's window on a whole world outside that has nothing to do with his or her parents. Best of all, grandmothers are subversive to parents without starting a rebellion and, as every kid knows instinctively, subversion is the grandest fun you can have.

My grandmother Hockenberry would stand in her kitchen, haul out box after box of cookies, candies, and confections and spread them all out before me. She would advise me not to eat everything in sight and make myself sick, advice I would never have taken at home. She would hand me a plate of goodies and open a family album to show me the pictures I never tired of seeing. I can remember the crumbs all over my face as we looked at sepia-toned snapshots of my father as a little boy fishing. She would point out the scab mark on his knee and point at the same perennial scab on my own knee. Most tantalizingly of all, she would wink at me and suggest that perhaps the first thing out of my mouth when I got home *not* be how many cookies Grandma had in her kitchen.

My grandmother Slagle would make lunch for my grandfather, who would come home from the office just in time for them to watch *Jeopardy* on TV. She would set up TV tables with place mats and napkins. There was a plate for a sand-

Doris Stryker Slagle with her husband, John Slagle.

wich, a bowl of soup, and some fruit salad. When I would stay with them Grandma would set up a tray just for me. My tray, plate, and chair were the same size as the adults'. I would sit there with my grandparents and try to answer the same questions they did and I would get a few myself. It was like being given the controls to a jet plane in flight. I was soloing as a grown-up there as a five year old sitting on a big dictionary in front of the TV answering questions about American History for 50 or Science for 100. My grand-mother was best with the movie questions and always deferred to me on anything having to do with science.

I grew up in a very large family: five kids, dogs, cats, fish. But my grandmother always spoke to me like I was the only person in the world. After my grandfather went back to the office, we washed the dishes together and she told me about all of the places my mother liked to play when she was little. During those afternoons, I would scout out the playgrounds of my mother and listen for her laughter. Through my grand-mother I could always hear it.

Even the word *grandmother* is mysterious to a child. It's the hardest word for a child to pronounce and the first task a child will persevere at solely for love, not survival. The word *grandmother* was way beyond me but I was determined to come up with some garbled equivalent. There must be some name that I could pronounce for this wonderful person with dazzling jewelry, white hair, and colorful dresses, who only existed, it seemed, to be my friend. Childhood names for grandparents often have a life of their own. In my family there was Gringa and Gringa (on my father's side), Nanna (both sides), and the elaborate Gee-Go-Gee and Ge-Go-Gee-Gah, which were my names for my grandparents on my mother's side. Great-grandmother was something else again. I always called my great-grandmother Me-Maw. The jolly old lady in the fluffy white blouses who lived upstairs at my grand-parents' house in Newark, New Jersey, was always Me-Maw. Once I coined this name it became what she preferred to be called. Even today, my parents refer to great-grandmother Slagle as Me-Maw.

Once when I was running around upstairs making too much noise, Me-Maw told me that I was just like my grand-father. Her words stopped me cold there in the hallway. "Do you mean that grandpa had to go to his room a lot?" I asked. Me-Maw looked down the hall. "He spent most of his child-hood there." There was a half-smile on her face. "Can I go there now?" I asked nearly trembling with excitement.

"Sure," she said and she took me down the hall to the room where I slept when I stayed with them in Newark. I went into that room and stared up at the ceiling. I laid down on the bed with one of the old books and quickly fell asleep. It was not really grandfather's room but my great-grandmother's words transported me back to a time when adults were children like me and I could imagine us all playing together on some black and white playground like in the pictures, where the old toys seemed bigger and were brand new.

I never realized it at the time but at my grandmother's I always went to my room on my own when I got too rambunctious, and never needed to be told to take an afternoon nap. And unlike being at home, it never felt like punishment.

Beatrice Eiche Hockenberry.

DREAMS

I know that whenever a group of women are gathered together, the grandmother always makes a phantom appearance, hovering above them.

–A<small>NGELA</small> C<small>ARTER</small>, <small>WRITER</small>

When I was about five, [my grandmother] told me years later, I crawled up in her ample lap and whispered my grandest dream in her ear. "Olma, I'm gonna be an actress. But don't tell Mother."

–F<small>AYE</small> D<small>UNAWAY</small>, <small>ACTRESS</small>
<small>ON HER</small> G<small>RANDMOTHER</small> O<small>LMA</small>

Teach the children. The Grandfathers and the Grandmothers are in the children. If we educated them, our children tomorrow will be wiser than we are today. They're the Grandfathers and Grandmothers of tomorrow.

–E<small>DDIE</small> B<small>ENTON</small>-B<small>ANIA</small>, O<small>JIBWAY ELDER</small>

TALKING TO MY GRANDMOTHER
WHO DIED POOR

(while hearing Richard Nixon declare "I am not a crook.")

no doubt i will end my life as poor as you
without the wide veranda of your dream
on which to sit and fan myself slowly
without the tall drinks to cool my bored
unthirsty throat.
you will think: Oh, my granddaughter failed
to make something of herself
in the White Man's World!

but i really am not a crook
i am not descended from crooks
my father was not president of anything
and only secretary to the masons
where his dues were a quarter a week
which he did not shirk to pay.

that buys me a new dream
though I may stray
and lust after jewelry
and a small house by the sea:
yet i could give up even lust
in proper times
and open my doors to strangers

or live in one room.
that is the new dream.

in the meantime i hang on
fighting addiction
to the old dream
knowing i must train myself to want
not one bit more
than what i need to keep me alive
working
and recognizing beauty
in your
        so nearly
undefeated face.

                              —ALICE WALKER

L ife is to be lived to its fullest so that death is just another
  chapter. Memories of our lives, our works and our deeds
will continue in others.

                    —ROSA PARKS, CIVIL RIGHTS PIONEER

Grandmother Guilia

*BY LUCIANO PAVAROTTI,
OPERA SINGER*

L uciano Pavarotti's grandmother told him] "One day, you're going to be great ... you will be ... you'll see." No teacher ever told me I would become famous. Just my grandmother. [She said] "Love people no matter what your occupation." Sometimes when I feel strange standing on stage, I ask myself: "What is little Luciano *doing* here?" I'm loving people—that's the key.

❧ —— ☙

Tempie LaBelle

BY PATTI LABELLE, SINGER

G randdaddy Henry loved my grandmother Tempie more than life itself. [Patti LaBelle's grandfather said to his young wife when she was stricken with leukemia] "Tempie, if I never see you again, if the Lord takes you, I won't live long behind you."

True love makes promises that can never be broken. Grandmother Tempie died in July 1938, and eight months later my grandfather was gone. The doctors said my grandfather died of a massive stroke. But people who knew them both tell a different story. Granddaddy Henry died of a broken heart.

Sometimes when I hear stories about Granddaddy Henry and Grandmother Tempie, I feel like crying. When I hear those stories, I realize just how much I have felt their absence in my life. Even so, there's one thing in this world I know for sure and for certain. My grandparents live on in me. All of our ancestors live on in each of us. People who knew Grandmother Tempie tell me that I sound just like her, that if they close their eyes when I'm singing, they could swear it's her voice they hear. She had the sweetest voice, my Aunt Hattie Mae told me. She was the church organist and people would come from miles around to hear her play and sing. Hattie Mae says the way she could hold a note and just let it float through the air would give you the chills. They called her "Mockingbird."

Anne Hayes

BY HELEN HAYES, ACTRESS (1900–1993)

Graddy Hayes was truly a remarkable woman, the strength of my young life. In Graddy's day women were considered old at fifty, and she was over sixty by the time I was born. Her hands were rough and red from years of housework, her hair gray, her wrinkles honorable signs of survival in a tough world.

Graddy loved the theatre and would scrimp and save in order to buy gallery tickets for plays presented in Washington by touring companies. Among the great actors we saw was Sarah Bernhardt, who performed in French. We didn't know a word of French, but Graddy claimed she could understand most everything because of Bernhardt's broad gestures and intonation. We also went to nickelodeon theatres to see silent movies featuring Maurice Costello, Florence Turner, and of Bronco Billy. Back home Graddy would act out a film we'd just seen, regaling the family with her mimicry, a talent she passed on to my mother and probably to me.

※ —— ✍

Minnie Mae and Claude Polk.

Minnie Mae Polk and Tillie Carter

BY DEANA CARTER, SINGER, SONGWRITER, AND MUSICIAN

My grandmothers were my mentors. Minnie Mae Polk was the most sweet-natured woman I have ever known. She is a descendant of the president James Polk. Her daughter, my mom, is just like her, gentle and compassionate. Grandma's kind-heartedness and generosity were well known in her town. She always left biscuits on her back porch for anyone who might need them. Hungry or homeless, they knew where to go. Though she died when I was still young, her legacy and example are with me always.

Tillie and Fred Carter Sr.

"You either make dust or you eat dust," Tillie Carter, my paternal grandmother, used to say. She was an incredible woman, full of spunk and character. She was also a ground-breaker on the radio in Louisiana. She had her own show at a tiny station. Tillie was involved in church music and filled her shows with gospel. My grandmother was the glue that held our family's interest in music together. We had a large family and, for Grandma, family and music were the focal points. She set the example we all followed. I am the third or fourth generation of musicians on my father's side of the family. I think my grandmother got her love of music from my great-grandfather. In my video for *Strawberry Wine,* there is a scene where I am standing in a door frame in a white slip. The slip once belonged to Tillie Carter. I held onto it all those years. She meant so much to me, I wanted to wear it in the video. My grandmother would be so happy to know what is happening with my career and in my life right now. As a matter of fact, I am sure she does.

꙳ —— ꙳

My grandmother was a fabulous woman who taught me to be strong and go for whatever I wanted in life. Her words of wisdom–"You can do it!" And I did!"

–JACKIE COLLINS, WRITER
ON HER GRANDMOTHER ROSALIND COLLINS

꙳ —— ꙳

Little Albert is such a dear good child that I already feel very sad when I think that I shall not see him again for quite a time. . . . We have fond recollections of little Albert. He was so dear and good, and we talk again and again of his droll ideas.

–JETTE KOCH, ALBERT EINSTEIN'S GRANDMOTHER
ON HER THEN TWO-YEAR-OLD GRANDSON (1881)

꙳ —— ꙳

Thelma Dawson

BY DIANA DAWSON, WRITER

As I curl with my little boy beneath a rose-and-gray afghan my Granny crocheted, I think of bedtime stories in which children's stuffed rabbits and nutcrackers and dolls magically come to life. I wish that in just the same way I could be granted one extra hour with the strongest woman I've ever known.

Granny and I would meet again in her two-story white farmhouse. It would be my favorite time of day with her, late in the afternoon after the new potatoes had been dug, the beans snapped, her sheets hung outside on the clothesline to dry and her iris beds weeded. She's sitting in her rocker and I am at the edge of the sofa on her right. Between us would be the end table that held my father's bronzed baby shoes, the lunch menu for the Vandalia Senior Citizens Center, and a tiny green photo album that began with Granny's special poem.

She'd rub some lotion into her arthritic fingers, but never tell me they hurt. Then we'd share one bottle of Mountain Dew, with lots of ice, in the same jelly-jar glasses she'd had since my father was a boy. I'd have a chance to ask her those nagging, big questions: Should I have one more baby? How can I tell as I'm searching for a new house whether it will be a home? If I got the nerve, I'd work up to the toughest question: "Will you forgive me for not being there often enough when you were dying?" . . .

I feel her love, steady as a leaky faucet. A love that was there when the boys didn't think I was cute enough to date and when my mother thought I was a sassy teenager. Long after I grew too old for lullabies I could still count on her singing a refrain of a song she'd adapted from her hymnal, "Granny loves you, this I know . . ." One hour. This is my wish. But unlike my son asleep beside me, I no longer expect magic.

On my night stand is Granny's little green album with the poem glued inside the cover. In our dining room is the table on which she served a lifetime of Thanksgiving turkeys and that pink Jell-O concoction she named "Diana's salad." I have the toy jar that sat on her step, the place where I always knew I could find the blue plastic motorcycle, the keys to her first home and a collection of wooden spools. My brother and I divided up the jelly-glass jars. But I haven't had a Mountain Dew since she left us.

In the darkness, my son's breathing is the only sound. Then, for a moment, I hear her voice, I imagine her singing "Granny loves you, this I know . . ." and finally, I feel at peace.

Grandmother Anna

BY PIPER LAURIE, ACTRESS

My grandmother Anna was still feisty and ambitious well into her nineties. She lived alone and began to disappear three days a week. Taking secret trips into downtown Los Angeles.

After many months she gave us a surprise accordion concert. Grandma had never played an instrument in her life.

What a great gift to know this woman was never afraid to try something new!

꙳ —— ꙳

Ada McGill

BY BARBARA MANDRELL, SINGER AND MUSICIAN

The first person ever to notice my music ability was not my father or my mother but Grandma Ada McGill back in Illinois. Grandma, who lived to be nearly a hundred, always remembered your name and recognized something about you, when somebody else might have needed a dog-gone scorecard to sort out all the children.

Grandma had a player piano in her house and she respected that old instrument so much that she would never let her grandkids beat away on it. But one day when I was three, I went and put my hands on the piano, and when Mommy and Daddy tried to stop me, Grandma said, "Let her alone, she's musically inclined." I wasn't playing anything that vaguely resembled a song, but Grandma heard something.

❧ —— ❧

Martha Pulliam

BY DAN QUAYLE,
FORMER U.S. VICE PRESIDENT

My grandmother was a pillar of strength and wisdom. As someone who was a single parent during an era when that was rare, she has always been to me the epitome of the single mother—independent, tireless, and completely family-centered. Her children and grandchildren grew up knowing that no one understood us better, loved us more, or believed in us more deeply. She remains one of the great influences of my life.

*A grandmother reading the morning paper
on the island of Santorini, Greece.*

Dona Sabina Quinn

BY ANTHONY QUINN, ACTOR

Antonio Moreno was the greatest Latin star in Hollywood. My grandmother never missed one of his pictures. She knew the storylines by heart, and could spin them into marvelous bedtime tales. There was only one movie house in El Paso.... To call it a theater was probably generous. It was little more than a large meeting room, raked, with folding bridge chairs set out in rows, but when the lights dimmed and the grainy picture flashed up on the screen, I was transported, just as my grandmother said I would be. There were horses and trains and strong-looking men. There was wild, bustling energy. I could not follow the story but my grandmother tried to explain it.

As I stared at the screen, the only sounds I heard were the whir of the projector and the rambling enthusiasm of my grandmother. "That could be you," she said, pointing to the screen. She whispered, even though there was no dialogue and no one to disturb. "Someday, you'll be bigger than Antonio Moreno. That's gonna be you. That's gonna be you. That's gonna be you."

I had no idea what she was talking about.

Obāchan

BY PATRICIA CHAO,
AUTHOR OF THE MONKEY KING

The grandmother I knew growing up was Japanese, my mother's mother, whom we called Obāchan. She was the matriarch of the family, a visionary who believed, in prewar Japan, that all women should be psychologically and financially independent. Two of my aunts are professional musicians, one is a poet, and my mother is a teacher and an entrepreneur. Obāchan herself was a member of a worldwide Christian missionary society.

When I was four and my brother two, Obāchan came to the United States to live with our family for a couple of years. I'll never forget my first sight of her–full-dress violet silk kimono, hair in an elaborate chignon, spotless white *tabi* (toe socks) and *zori*. But she turned out to be a regular grandmother, who cooked, comforted, and told bedtime stories, although hers were Japanese folktales.

What I remember most vividly about my grandmother and what formed a bond between us was something I grew to appreciate when I was older–her unique sense of style. No one could wear clothes–kimono, Chanel, or the plainest housedress–like Obāchan. Her greatest vanity was her elegant hands, and she wore gloves more and more often as she got older. For reasons of her own, she singled me out as the prettiest granddaughter and the one most malleable to her fashion sense. In any case, it was heady stuff for a too-tall, awkward wallflower like me. When our family went to Tokyo to visit, my grandmother would greet me with "Oh, you're so lovely!" followed by a barrage of criticism and suggestions: "That's the wrong collar for your face." "You should always wear hats." "Don't you ever iron your pants?" (I'd be wearing jeans.) She was always buying me things—a teal-green disco dress slit up the side, which scandalized my mother; the snow-white satin kimono set with obi and the quilted jacket she sent from Japan for my wedding many years later, when she was too ill to make the trip herself.

The last time I saw her was a couple of years before that in Tokyo. I had stopped en route to Beijing, where I had a job editing English the year after I graduated from college. We went clothes shopping (she bought me a red Tyrolean hat), took a Japanese bath together, and she told me a strange story that she said she'd never breathed to any living soul, including my mother. It had to do with a lost brother and traveling by herself to Shanghai when she was twenty years old to look after him.

In many ways my grandmother remains a mystery and a myth to me, although my mother says I have her hands: I'm the only one in the family to have inherited them. Over the years I've amassed quite a glove collection—kid, cotton, silk, chiffon; you could say that they used to be my trademark, although I rarely wear them nowadays. There will come a time, I'm sure, when, like my grandmother, I'll go back to gloves for coverage rather than fashion statement. But for now, some perverse part of me likes watching my naked hands–leaner and more tendony as they age–turn into Obāchan's.

FACES
(excerpt)

Behold a woman!
She looks out from her Quaker cap, her face is clearer and
    more beautiful than the sky.
She sits in an armchair under the shaded porch of the
    farmhouse,
The sun just shines on her old white head.
Her ample gown is of cream-hued linen,
Her grandsons raised the flax, and her granddaughters spin
    it with the distaff and the wheel.
The melodious character of the earth,
The finish beyond which philosophy cannot go and does
    not wish to go,
The justified mother of men.

–WALT WHITMAN

Vincenzo and Maria Antonia Imprescia

Maria Antonia Imprescia

BY JUDITH REGAN, PRESIDENT AND PUBLISHER, REGANBOOKS, AND HOST OF FOX NEWS CHANNEL'S THAT REGAN WOMAN

S he never went to school.
  She couldn't read.

She could barely write her own name.

Her mother died in childbirth when she was two years old. Because her family could not afford a wet nurse, the infant died of starvation. It was 1889 in a small, primitive village in the foothills of Mount Etna, Sicily. A long way from the invention of formula and baby bottles.

My grandmother and her siblings, all under the age of six, wandered the streets while her father picked olives from sunup to sundown.

She was two years old and what would be described today as a street urchin. After her father died, this young teenager came to America, an indentured servant without an education, without a family, to work as a maid. She later worked in a factory, where she met her husband-to-be.

Together, they raised seven children during the Great Depression, with little or no money, long periods of unemployment, in what would be described today as utter poverty.

I was raised in that same house. My grandparents lived downstairs. And although no one ever had any money, I had an enchanting childhood, filled with the *smell* of freshly baked bread (I'd spend one afternoon a week kneading gobs of dough with my grandmother); the *sight* of enormous gardens filled with flowers, fruits, and vegetables (we spent hours in the garden, where she taught me the name of each plant and how to care for it); and the *feel* of her constant warm embraces and smothering kisses.

She was petite, but her kindness and generosity were grand. Whenever we had company—and this was a large family, so there was plenty of company—one simple principle applied. We were always to give our best tomatoes, our finest roses, the most beautiful peaches or grapes. And if it was winter, you gave the best of your cheese, your meats, your freshly baked bread or thick-crusted pizza, the bottles of your homemade root beer filled with the most delicious, syrupy liquid, hot off the stove.

You gave your best and you gave it at all times. And sometimes that meant you did without, or you ate the rotten tomatoes, but it always meant that you cared and you demonstrated that care by giving.

My grandmother died when I was nineteen years old. She was in her eighties and was still living at home, caring for her son, who was half-paralyzed and brain damaged. She had seen several of her children die, her husband die, and most of her other children move away.

Today, almost twenty-five years after her death, she would be called a poor, illiterate immigrant.

I have traveled worldwide, met world leaders, brilliant scholars, media moguls, Hollywood stars, and religious leaders. I run a publishing company, a television and film production company, and I host my own television talk show.

I have never met anyone who influenced me and taught me more than my grandmother, a woman I called "Ma."

Today, my twenty-ninth-floor midtown Manhattan office windows are lined with pots of various flowers and even tomato plants.

One pot bears the long, slender stems of a scallion plant that originally bloomed in the soil of my grandmother's Sicilian homeland.

He's a chatterbox. He's a chatterbox. He's going to be on television."

–AL ROKER, TV WEATHERMAN
QUOTING HIS GRANDMOTHER

❧ —— ☙

Pauline Perlmutter Steinem

BY GLORIA STEINEM,
CONSULTING EDITOR, MS. MAGAZINE

My paternal grandmother died when I was five, so my sense of her came mainly through family stories about her accomplishments as a homemaker, pioneer of vocational education, and mother of four sons.

It wasn't until a feminist scholar wrote a monograph about her that I realized Pauline Perlmutter Steinem had been more of a rebel than those stories implied. She was a suffragist who attended international women's meetings, and addressed Congress as part of the campaign for the vote. The first woman elected to the school board in Toledo, Ohio, she not only ran on a coalition ticket with the anarchists and the socialists, but defeated the efforts of gangs of men and boys to keep women away from the polls–using what we might now call sexual harassment—because she organized women to vote *together*.

Now, I remember her not only for her own courage, but as a symbol of the ways women's history can be lost, even in the most well-meaning of families. Perhaps a grandmother or aunt or cousin—the one the family doesn't speak of, or the part of her life left out of family stories—is the courageous example we need most to learn.

❧ —— ❦

Molly Horniblow

BY HARRIET ANN JACOBS, WRITER (1813–1897)

I was born a slave; but I never knew it till six years of happy childhood passed away. I was so fondly shielded that I never dreamed I was a piece of merchandise, trusted to them (the owners) for safe keeping, and liable to be demanded of them at any moment. I had a great treasure in my maternal grandmother, who was remarkable in many respects. I have often heard her tell how hard she fared during childhood. But as she grew older she evinced so much intelligence, and was so faithful, that her master and mistress could not help seeing it was for their interest to take care of such a valuable piece of property. She became an indispensable personage in the household, officiating in all capacities, from cook and wet nurse to seamstress. She was much praised for her cooking; and her nice crackers became so famous in the neighborhood that many people were desirous of obtaining them. In consequence of numerous requests of this kind, she asked permission of her mistress to bake crackers at night, after all the housework was done; and she obtained leave to do it, provided she would clothe herself and her children from the profits. . . . To this good grandmother I was indebted for many comforts. My brother Willie and I often received portions of the crackers, cakes, and preserves, she made to sell; and after we ceased to be children we were indebted to her for many more important services. . . .

Little attention was paid to the slaves' meals in Dr. Flint's house. If they could catch a bit of food while it was going, well and good. I gave myself no trouble on that score, for on my various errands I passed my grandmother's house, where there was always something to spare for me. I was frequently threatened with punishment if I stopped there; and my grandmother to avoid detaining me, often stood at the gate with something for my breakfast or my dinner. I was indebted to *her* for all my comforts, spiritual or temporal. It was *her* labor that supplied my scanty wardrobe.

[Harriet Jacobs managed to escape to the North.] From time to time I received news from my good old grandmother. She could not write; but she employed others to write for her. The following is an extract from one of her last letters—

*Dear Daughter: I cannot hope to see you again on earth;
but I pray to God to unite us above, where pain will no
more rack this feeble body of mine; where sorrow and
parting from my children will be no more. God has promised
these things if we are faithful unto the end. My age and
feeble health deprive me of going to church now; but God is
with me here at home. Thank your brother for his kindness.
Give much love to him, and tell him to remember the Creator in the days of his youth, and strive to meet me in the
Father's kingdom. Love to Ellen and Benjamin. Don't
neglect him. Tell him for me, to be a good boy. Strive, my
child, to train them for God's children. May he protect and
provide for you, is the prayer of your loving old mother.*

These letters both cheered and saddened me. I was
always glad to have tidings from the kind, faithful old friend
of my unhappy youth; but her messages of love made my
heart yearn to see her before she died, and I mourned over
the fact that it was impossible. . . . I remembered how my
good old grandmother had laid up her earnings to purchase
me in later years, and how often her plans had been frustrated. How that faithful, loving old heart would leap for joy,
if she could look on me and my children now that we were
free!

My grandmother lived to rejoice in my freedom; but not
long after, a letter came with a black seal. She had gone
"where the wicked cease from troubling, and the weary are
at rest."

Reader, my story ends with freedom; not in the usual way, with marriage. I and my children are now free! ... It has been painful to me, in many ways, to recall the dreary years I passed in bondage. I would gladly forget them if I could. Yet the retrospection is not altogether without solace; for with those gloomy recollections come tender memories of my good old grandmother, like light, fleecy clouds over a dark troubled sea.

~ AFTERWORD ~

Sixty years ago, decades before feminism even entered the American vocabulary, Mary May Bell found herself married to a professional gambler with two small children to feed. When money was plentiful, there was food on the table. But when her husband's luck ran out, so did the groceries. Unwilling to raise her children under these conditions, Mary Bell advised her husband, "I cannot live not knowing if the children will have milk tomorrow. I am not putting up with a man who doesn't respect his family." With that, she did something unheard of in those days—she divorced him. If her husband was not going to provide a stable home for her children, she would. And she did.

With limited training and experience, my grandmother took a job on the night shift working the hydraulic pumps at a railroad crossing. This was a position many men considered beneath them, but not my grandmother. She believed in the dignity of work—all work, whether you were a CEO or

Mary May Bell.

cleaning toilets. All honest work was dignified because you were taking care of yourself and your family, and there was nothing more important than that. Furthermore, no one, man or woman, need be dependent on anyone else for their well-being or world view. My grandmother never forgot who she was and she never pretended to be anyone else.

Grandma would arrive promptly for her shift, immaculately groomed, with her powder and lipstick intact. She wasn't out to impress anyone. After all, there was rarely anyone around *to* impress on the night shift. But Grandma never left the house without her powder and lipstick. It was a matter of personal pride and respect. Anyone who thinks putting on lipstick and powder is frivolous didn't know my grandmother. She was proud to be a woman. Later, when the women's movement burgeoned in the sixties, I felt little identification with it. I had always felt liberated as a woman.

Grandma used to say, "When you look in the mirror, the one you have to answer to is yourself, so you better like what you see, both inside and out. And remember, there are mirrors everywhere, in your family, colleagues, friends and neighbors, as well as the ones that hang on the wall. You must always be able to look into your own eyes. You will make mistakes and that is all right, as long as you strive to live up to the standards you have set for yourself." When I was young, I sometimes went to work with Grandma and slept on the floor in the railroad shanty to be near her. Without her example, I don't think I ever would have put myself through college. But I learned self-reliance early. I learned that as long as you were willing to believe in yourself and work hard, no goal was impossible. So I did everything from wait tables to take in laundry, and I earned my college degree. In a material sense, our family didn't have much. We lived on the edge of poverty in a small Indiana steel town, but I had what every girl should have: unconditional love, support, and the finest of role models.

My grandmother had been blessed with similar advantages. Her mother was just like her. My great-grandfather died, leaving my great-grandmother with four children to raise alone. The day after his death, my great-grandmother silently walked into the plant where her husband had worked for years, punched in, and assumed his place on the assembly line. No employee records were adjusted, no words were said. With a family to feed, a position to fill, and dignity, BaBa, my great-grandmother, stepped in.

In September 1996, Mary May Bell died peacefully in her sleep at the age of ninety-three. She was one of the most extraordinary women I have ever known, and her legacy lives on in those of us who loved her.

GEORGETTE MOSBACHER

COPYRIGHT ACKNOWLEDGMENTS

Press, Berkeley, California, 1995). Reprinted by permission of Valerie Kack-Brice.

Kuralt, Charles. *Always the First Lady: Eleanor Roosevelt.* Copyright © 1996 by Charles Kuralt. Reprinted by permission of The New York Times, Inc.

LaBelle, Patti. *Don't Block the Blessings* by Patti LaBelle (Riverhead Books, a division of Putnam Publishing). Copyright © 1996 Patti LaBelle. Reprinted by permission of Riverhead Books, a division of Putnam Publishing.

Mandrell, Barbara. *Get to the Heart* by Barbara Mandrell with George Vecsey (Bantam Books, Inc.). Copyright © Barbara Mandrell. Reprinted by permission of Bantam Books, a division of Bantam Doubleday Dell Publishing Group, Inc.

Markova, Dawna. *For She Is the Tree of Life: Grandmothers through the Eyes of Women Writers* edited by Valerie Kack-Brice (Conari Press, Berkeley, California, 1995). Reprinted by permission of Dawna Markova.

Martinez, Victor. *Parrot in the Oven mi vida.* Copyright © 1996, Victor Martinez. Reprinted by permission of Joanna Cotler Books, HarperCollins Publishers, Inc.

Mateer, Carolyn. *For She Is the Tree of Life: Grandmothers through the Eyes of Women Writers* edited by Valerie Kack-Brice (Conari Press, Berkeley, California, 1995). Reprinted by permission of Carolyn Mateer.

Mead, Margaret. *Blackberry Winter* by Margaret Mead (William Morrow and Company, Inc.). Copyright © 1972 by Margaret Mead. Reprinted by permission of William Morrow and Company, Inc.

Miller, Joshua. *The Mao Game* (ReganBooks, An imprint of HarperCollins Publishers, 1997). Copyright © 1997 Joshua Miller. Reprinted by permission of ReganBooks, HarperCollins Publishers.

Nixon, Richard. *The Memoirs of Richard Nixon* (Grosset & Dunlap Publishers, New York).

Oliver, Mary. *No Voyage and Other Poems* (Houghton Mifflin). Copyright © 1965, 1993 by Mary Oliver. Reprinted by permission of the Molly Malone Cook Literary Agency.

Plaskin, Glenn. *Turning Points: Pivotal Moments in the Lives of America's Celebrities* by Glenn Plaskin (Birch Lane Press, Carol Publishing 1992). Copyright © 1992 by Glenn Paskin. Reprinted by permission of Birch Lane Press, Carol Publishing Group.

Pollitzer, Anita. *A Woman on Paper: Georgia O'Keeffe.* Copyright © 1988, The Estate of Anita Pollitzer. Reprinted by permission of Simon & Schuster, Inc.

Quinn, Anthony. *One Man Tango* by Anthony Quinn, with Daniel Paisner. (HarperCollins Publishers, 1995). Copyright © 1995 by Anthony Quinn with Daniel Paisner. Reprinted by permission of HarperCollins Publishers, Inc.

Rebennack, Mac (Dr. John) with Jack Rummel, *Under a Hoodoo Moon: The Life of Dr. John the Night Tripper*, by Mac (Dr. John) Rebennack with Jack Rummel. Copyright © 1994 by Mac Rebennack. Reprinted by permission of St. Martin's Press Inc.

Walker, Alice. *Goodnight, Willie Lee, I'll See You in the Morning.* Copyright © 1974, Alice Walker. Reprinted by permission of Doubleday, Bantam Doubleday Dell Publishing Group, Inc.

Walker, Margaret. *Lineage* by Margaret Walker. Copyright © Margaret Walker. Reprinted by permission of Margaret Walker.

Wharton, Edith. *A Backward Glance.* Copyright © 1933, 1934, William R. Tyler; renewal copyright © 1961, 1962. Reprinted by permission of Scribner, a division of Simon & Schuster, Inc.

PHOTOGRAPHY PERMISSIONS

Photograph of Grandma Moses reprinted courtesy of Warner Wolf Black Star.

Photograph of the Judds reprinted courtesy of Lynn Self.

Photograph of Michael Dorris reprinted courtesy of Lee Fagin.

All additional photographs reprinted by permission of contributors.